CELEBRATIONS

DELICIOUS RECIPES ✦ HEARTWARMING STORIES
HOLIDAY DECOR ✦ FUN CRAFTS

ISBN 978-1-62145-787-9 (dated)
ISBN 978-1-62145-788-6 (undated)

Component Number 117200104H (dated)
117200106H (undated)

We are committed to both the quality of our products and the service we provide to our customers. We value your comments, so please feel free to contact us at TMBBookTeam@TrustedMediaBrands.com.

Printed In China.
1 3 5 7 9 10 8 6 4 2

Text, photography and illustrations for *Country Woman Celebrations: Spring/Summer 2022* are based on articles previously published in *Country Woman*, *Country*, *Farm & Ranch Living*, and *Reminisce* magazines.

NOTE TO OUR READERS

The editors who produced this book have attempted to make the contents as accurate and correct as possible. Illustrations, photographs and text have been carefully checked. All instructions should be reviewed and understood by the reader before undertaking any project. The directions and designs for the projects in this publication are under copyright. These projects may be reproduced for the reader's personal use or for gifts. Reproduction for sale or profit is forbidden by law.

Credits

v, 164 loraleelewis.com; **vi-1, 24** Megan Fuss Photography; **3** Crafted by Stephanie Sliwinski/Fancy That Design House & Co.; **7** Craft by Dottie Blatz; **9, 10, 11** Krista Aasen/thehappyhousie.com; **19, 20** Jerrelle Guy; **22** Breanna Smith; **31, 138** Crafted by Samantha Bender/Pleasantly Crafted; **38, 39** *t* George Flynn; **62, 169** Produced and Photographed by Matthew Mead; **64, 65, 224** Andrew Ricchiuti; **67** istock.com/imgorthand; **72** Craft by Alison Auth; **84** Jacquie McTaggert; **86, 87** Brandee Moore; **91, 137** Crafted by Sarah Bierstedt/Purple Pincushion; **100** Illustration by Gary Hovland; **102, 103** Amie Rolland; **108** Crafted by Sarah Vanderkooy; **112-115** Melissa Yocum; **130** Janis Parr; **132** Devonp Photography; **154** Kristen Wineinger; **155** Jenna Stevens; **156** *b* Harriet Gilleland; **157** Terry Wild/Terry Wild Stock; **158** Paul Rezendes; **159** Gerry Eisert; **159** Shirley Stuby; **161** Illustration by Daniel Downey; **166** Bachman's; **167** *t* Hirschfield's; **167** *b* Brenda Barr; **186** Illustration by Gary Hovland; **188** Illustration by Gian Livado; **192** Craft by Vanessa Tsumura; **194** Craft by Jane Craig; **208, 209** Donna Zacharias; **Back cover** *tl*, 213 Aneeta Brown

Getty Images: background throughout Olgastocker; **129** Nat and Cody Gantz; **156** *t* Bill Chizek
Shutterstock: 39 *b* Kostin SS; **68** spfotocz

Table of Contents

It's Party Time!

There's nothing like a little down-home country resourcefulness to help you celebrate in style! In this book, you'll find recipes, craft projects and decorating tips for all your spring and summer festivities.

Dress up old plastic Easter eggs with twine. Welcome Dad home on Father's Day with a wreath made of his old ties. Treat Mom to Cast-Iron Scrambled Eggs and Chocolate Bread for a proper Mother's Day brunch. Decorate your Fourth of July bash with Star Lights and Firecracker Napkins. Laugh at the story of the pie and the preacher.

From do-it-yourself decorations and party favors to cherished traditions and the sweetest treats, the best holiday memories are made in the country.

—The Editors of *Country Woman*

Spring

Crafts and Decor

Recipes

Stories

Handkerchief Table Runner

End-to-end hankies are a distinctive and dainty way to top a table.

WHAT YOU'LL NEED

- Vintage handkerchiefs
- Coordinating thread
- Coordinating lace trim
- Coordinating ribbon trim
- Sewing machine or sewing needle
- Fabric shears

DIRECTIONS

1. Lay handkerchiefs side by side to reach desired length. Pin them into place.
2. If using a sewing machine, sew 1 handkerchief onto the next. If using a needle and thread, use a running stitch to sew handkerchiefs together by hand.
3. Using fabric shears, cut 2 pieces of lace the length of the runner's ends. Pin 1 piece of lace to the back side of each end. Sew lace trim behind the handkerchief ends.
4. Cut 2 pieces of ribbon trim the length of the runner's ends. Pin 1 piece of ribbon trim to the front side of each end. Stitch ribbon in place.

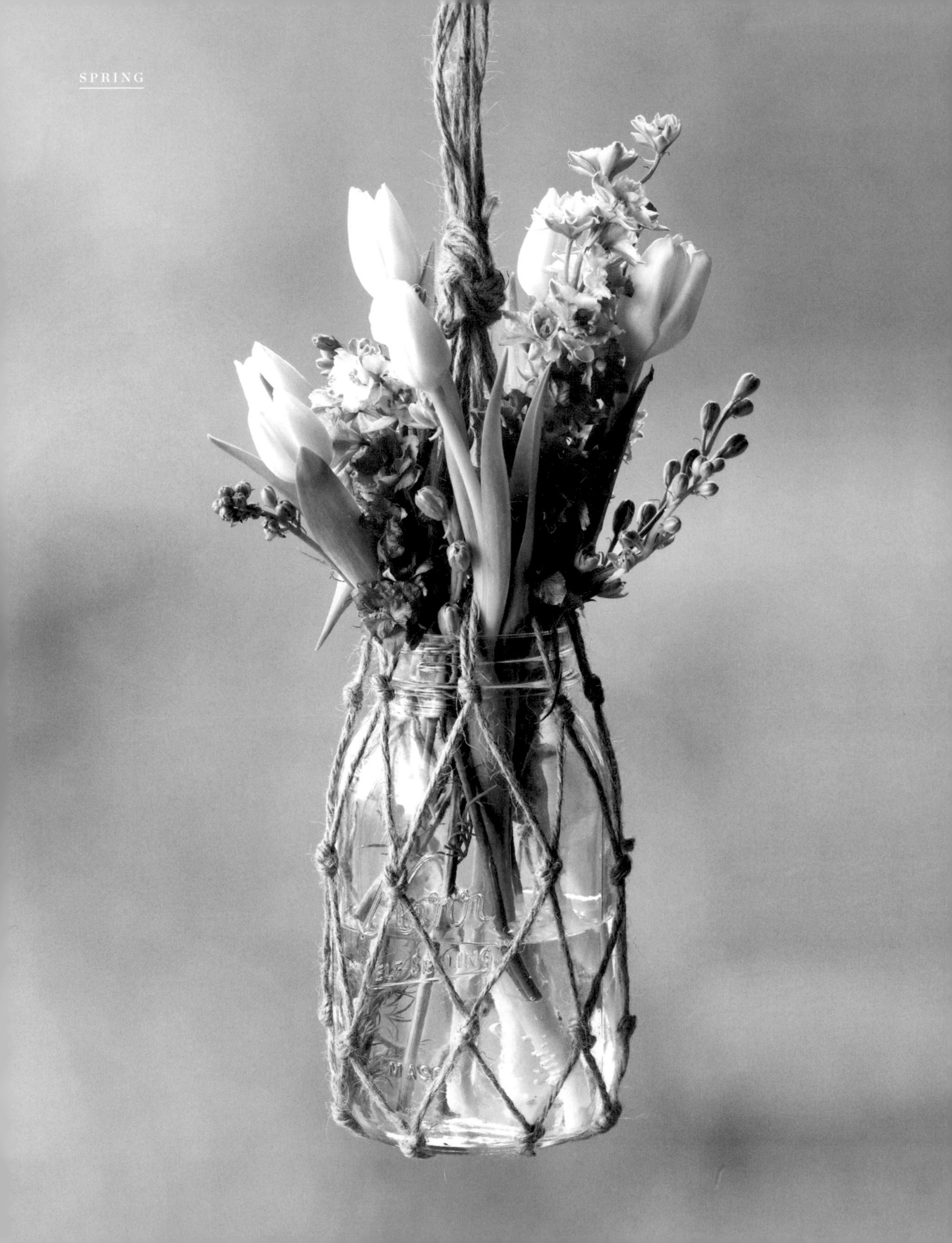

Knotted Hanging Vase

Old-fashioned macrame returns
with a fresh twist.

WHAT YOU'LL NEED

- **32 ft. of 2 mm jute twine**
- **Quart-size mason jar**

DIRECTIONS

1. Cut twine into 8 equal pieces. Group in 2 bundles of 4 pieces.
2. Lay the 2 bundles perpendicular to each other, crossing them in the middle. Tie them in a lanyard knot (see page 214).
3. Separate 2 strands from 2 side-by-side bundles. Tie them in a knot 1½ in. above the lanyard knot. Repeat all the way around, until all the strands have been tied together.
4. Move another 1½ in. above the first row of knots and tie 2 more strands together, making sure to pull the strands from side-by-side knots and not the same section. This will create the diamond-shaped pattern. Repeat all the way around again.
5. Continue the pattern for 5 rows of knots. Gather the excess twine at the top and tie in a thick knot to use to hang the vase. Insert the mason jar, centering the bottom on the lanyard knot, and fill as desired.

Leaf Birdbath

Capture the natural beauty of a large leaf in this
elegant, do-it-yourself cement birdbath.

WHAT YOU'LL NEED

- Large leaf
- Bag of play sand
- 3-4 cups masonry sand
- 1-2 cups Portland cement
- Concrete fortifier
- Hand pruners

- Plastic sheet
- 2 plastic bowls
- Masonry paint (the type
  intended for swimming pools)
  or clear sealer, optional
- Paintbrush, optional

DIRECTIONS

1. Cut the stem off a leaf that is at least 10 in. long and 7 in. wide.

2. Cut a piece of plastic sheet slightly larger than the leaf. Set aside. Cover work surface with the rest of the plastic sheet. Pour play sand onto the plastic in a pile, wetting it slightly so it sticks together.

3. Shape the sand into the approximate size and shape of the leaf, keeping in mind birds do not like baths that are more than a couple of inches deep. Cover shaped sand with reserved sheet. Place the leaf vein side up on the plastic.

4. In a plastic bowl, mix 3 parts masonry sand to 1 part Portland cement. In a separate bowl, mix ¼ cup water with ¼ cup concrete fortifier; add slowly to sand mixture until it reaches the consistency of thick brownie batter, mixing and adding more water and fortifier if needed.

5. Place a handful of the mixture on the center of the leaf, spreading it to the edge.

6. Build up the thickness of the casting until it reaches ½-1 in. thick. Take care to keep the edges smooth to get a good contour. Build up the center to make a base.

7. Cover loosely with plastic. Let dry for about 24 hours, then peel off the leaf. If the casting feels brittle, let it sit for another day.

8. If you want to paint or seal the birdbath, let it first cure for a week.

 Tip To keep your birdbath from cracking during winter's freeze-thaw cycles, consider bringing it inside during colder months.

Water Colors

Bring the joys of lake life home—no matter where you live—with this wave of easy, breezy ideas.

BY RACHAEL LISKA

Water—humans are drawn to it. From deep, dark blue mountain lakes to picturesque ponds of glassy green, water is quite literally a part of us. No wonder it's inspired coastlines of cabins along Lake Superior and quaint camps nestled next to rushing woodland streams. Now add the Happy Housie's Krista Aasen's home to the list.

Krista and her family live on the crystal-clear freshwater Sproat Lake on Vancouver Island in British Columbia. The watercolor walls of their cozy coastal cottage are a testament to how lake living has complemented Krista's decorating sensibilities.

"Being waterfront has definitely influenced my color scheme, but since this is our full-time home, I've tried to create a subtle coastal feel without being too theme-y," says Krista, who blogs about her designs at thehappyhousie.com.

As a kindergarten teacher, wife and mom of two active young boys, Krista knows well how to balance a house's fashion and function.

"Nowhere in our home is off-limits to the boys," says Krista. "They hang out and watch TV in the living room, and the hallway is often used for mini hockey games or pitching practice."

To keep the look family-casual yet chic, Krista mixes vintage finds and DIY projects with high-style newer pieces. "Paint and DIY paneling are my biggest tips for adding character and drama to a space while staying on budget. I also love a well-placed, colorfully painted vintage piece like our coffee table. And the map wallpaper was an almost-free DIY project

Right: Krista Aasen pulls the calm blue tones of a nearby lake into her home.

that adds huge impact to our entryway."

This mix can be seen in the living room, where thrift-store finds like an oversized cheese box turned into a side table mingle with an elegant linen-covered sofa with nail-head trim from Wayfair. In the dining room, vintage artwork in Krista's favorite colors—blue, aqua, turquoise and teal—and a repurposed church pew mix with new dining room chairs and a modern chandelier.

"I think an eclectic mix of old and new gives a home its character," she says. ♦

....

Bottom: Krista Aasen's father built the farmhouse-style table in her dining room. Right: Wood planking on the kitchen island and the wooden range hood are DIY projects that add drama without a lot of cost.

1. MAKE A GOOD FIRST IMPRESSION

"In an entryway, I like to include a spot to place keys, hooks to hang up coats or bags, and a chair so guests can sit while they put on their shoes," Krista says.

2. GET CREATIVE WITH COLOR

"I love to add colors that feel appropriate to the season, while working within our main scheme of watery blues and greens. In spring, I throw in a bit of pink or purple along with fresh pastels."

3. PRACTICE SEASONAL STYLE

"My favorite way to change our decor seasonally is to switch out my throw pillows and blankets."

Pork Loin with Strawberry-Rhubarb Chutney

I love strawberry-rhubarb pie, so I thought the same flavor combination could work as a chutney—and it does! This makes a delicious and festive accompaniment to a succulent pork roast.

—Deborah Biggs, Omaha, NE

Prep **20 min.** ◆ Bake **1 hour + standing** ◆ Makes **10 servings (1¾ cups sauce)**

WHAT YOU'LL NEED

- 1 boneless pork loin roast (3 to 4 lbs.)
- 1 tsp. salt
- ½ tsp. pepper
- 2 Tbsp. canola oil
- ½ cup sugar
- ¼ cup red wine vinegar
- 1 cinnamon stick (3 in.)
- ½ tsp. grated lemon zest
- 2¼ cups chopped fresh or frozen rhubarb
- ⅔ cup sliced fresh strawberries
- 1½ tsp. minced fresh rosemary or ½ tsp. dried rosemary, crushed

DIRECTIONS

1. Sprinkle roast with salt and pepper. In a large skillet, brown roast in oil on all sides.

2. Place roast on a rack in a shallow roasting pan. Bake, uncovered, at 350° until a thermometer reads 145°, 1-1½ hours. Remove roast to a serving platter; let stand for 15 minutes.

3. Meanwhile, in a large saucepan, combine sugar, vinegar, cinnamon and lemon zest. Bring to a boil. Reduce heat; simmer, uncovered, until sugar is dissolved, about 2 minutes.

4. Add rhubarb, strawberries and rosemary. Cook and stir over medium heat until rhubarb is tender and mixture is slightly thickened, 15-20 minutes. Discard cinnamon stick and serve with pork.

4 OZ. COOKED PORK WITH 3 TBSP. CHUTNEY 243 cal., 9g fat (3g sat. fat), 68mg chol., 277mg sod., 13g carb. (11g sugars, 1g fiber), 27g pro. **DIABETIC EXCHANGES** 3 lean meat, ½ fruit, ½ fat.

 Tip The chutney can be made a day ahead and kept in the refrigerator.

Zesty Sugar Snap Peas

Lemon-pepper seasoning and garlic make these crisp-tender sugar snap peas an ideal complement to a variety of entrees.

—Taste of Home *Test Kitchen*

Takes **15 min.** ◆ Makes **4 servings**

WHAT YOU'LL NEED

- **1** lb. fresh or frozen sugar snap peas
- **1** Tbsp. butter
- **1** garlic clove, minced
- **¾** tsp. lemon-pepper seasoning
- **¼** tsp. salt

DIRECTIONS

In a skillet, bring peas and ½ cup water to a boil. Reduce heat. Cover and cook until tender, 6-7 minutes. Drain. Add remaining ingredients. Cook and stir until well-coated, 2-3 minutes.

¾ **CUP** 74 cal., 3g fat (2g sat. fat), 8mg chol., 267mg sod., 8g carb. (4g sugars, 3g fiber), 4g pro. **DIABETIC EXCHANGES** 1 vegetable, ½ fat.

Simple Lemon Mousse

This classic, simple mousse is the refreshing dessert you need. Serve it with fresh fruit or eat it alone.

—Taste of Home *Test Kitchen*

Prep **20 min.** ◆ Cook **10 min.** + chilling ◆ Makes **6 servings**

WHAT YOU'LL NEED

- ⅔ cup sugar
- 2 Tbsp. cornstarch
  Dash salt
- 3 large egg yolks
- ⅔ cup whole milk
- ½ cup lemon juice
- 2 tsp. grated lemon zest
- 1 cup heavy whipping cream
  Lemon slices, optional

DIRECTIONS

1. In a small saucepan, mix sugar, cornstarch and salt; whisk in egg yolks and milk until smooth. Whisk in lemon juice until blended; bring to a boil over medium heat, stirring constantly. Cook and stir until thickened slightly, 2 minutes longer. Stir in lemon zest.
2. Transfer mixture to a bowl. Cover and refrigerate until cold.
3. To serve, in a small bowl, beat cream on high speed until soft peaks form. Fold into lemon mixture. Spoon into serving dishes. If desired, top with additional whipped cream and lemon slices.

½ **CUP** 282 cal., 18g fat (11g sat. fat), 140mg chol., 52mg sod., 29g carb. (25g sugars, 0 fiber), 3g pro.

Baking with the Senses

In this precise art, the fun is found
by feeling your way through.

BY JERRELLE GUY

Rules and precision aren't naturally my thing. I'm a hypersensitive baker, preferring to get lost in the smells and textures of the food and the sizzling sounds they make while boiling in a saucepan or roasting under an oven's coil. So, in this way, I'm not the baker you might expect; I've never studied under some tough-as-nails patissier in France to survive and tell the tale, and I also have really hot hands, which is a curse when I'm trying to work cold butter into flour before it turns to mush.

But my grandmother was a resilient baker—resourceful, intuitive and smart, and something that just recently dawned on me is that she never used a kitchen scale. Yet every Sunday her biscuits were spot on, so tender and ready to be split to lie beneath a hard scramble of peppered eggs. May she rest in peace.

After realizing that, I started to appreciate how much of the baking process is learning the way food and ingredients should behave—the proper thickness of a yellow cake batter when my spoon is lifted, the smell of fruit when it's ripe enough to bake, the correct tackiness of dough for the bread or pastry I'm kneading—and how to set these things right if they're not already. It's something

For years, Jerrelle Guy baked without a scale, choosing instead to rely on her senses to know when batters and doughs were just right.

that just comes with years of practice—and failure.

I'd never even thought about getting a scale until I wanted to start baking for other people: for my fluky cookie business post-graduation and when I agreed to write a cookbook. I froze up, started second-guessing myself and wondered whether everything I made had a texture that would please the baking gods. But boy, I tell you, life before those times was heavenly as I happily munched away at whatever unmeasured, off-the-cuff pie I threw together, and friends and family close enough to steal a slice would rave.

While there definitely are tips I've lifted from books and YouTube videos that help me understand why a cake collapsed or made my mouth pucker (too much baking soda, perhaps?), part of me enjoys making a fool of myself on the first go-round while botching a batch of whatever recipe it is I've dared to change and ruin. It is a moment of masochism that makes room for a flood of big waves of happiness and pride when it does come out perfectly and I've invented something new.

For many desserts, a recipe can do only so much anyway. Flour, eggs, ovens—they can all be so persnickety, can't they? I remember my first time trying to whip egg whites into lush meringue. It was a disaster. I spent weeks trying to get "silky stiff peaks"—whatever that meant. It wasn't until I failed close to 10 times, and moved away from the balmy Texas air, that I understood what silky, stiff peaks

actually were, what they felt like on my fingers and roughly how long my beater had to run until they got there.

I will offer you all the exact weight measurements I use, but I also encourage you to stop along the way to savor the sounds, colors, textures and smells that I noticed while writing them down. For me, that's all the fun. ♦

Reprinted with permission from Black Girl Baking by Jerrelle Guy, Page Street Publishing Co. 2018

Chocolate, Chocolate Veneer Cake

I don't have a big taste for dense sugar-saturated icings. I keep this icing fluffy, cold, thin and just sweet enough.

—*Jerrelle Guy, Boston, MA*

Prep **20 min.** ◆ Bake **30 min.** ◆ Makes **One 9-inch layer cake**

WHAT YOU'LL NEED

- 2 cups white whole wheat flour
- ⅔ cup cocoa powder
- 1½ tsp. baking powder
- 1 tsp. baking soda
- 1 tsp. salt
- 1¼ cups sugar
- 1 cup buttermilk
- ½ cup canola oil
- 1 Tbsp. vanilla extract
- 1 cup hot coffee

ICING

- 1 cup dairy-free semisweet chocolate chips, melted
- 3 Tbsp. coconut oil
- 1 can (15 oz.) coconut cream, chilled in refrigerator overnight
- Fresh berries, optional

DIRECTIONS

1. Preheat oven to 350°. Line two 8-inch greased cake pans with parchment. Place metal bowl in freezer.
2. Stir together flour, cocoa powder, baking powder, baking soda and salt in a bowl.
3. In a separate bowl, whisk sugar, buttermilk, oil and vanilla until smooth. Sift dry ingredients into wet ingredients; fold gently. Whisk in coffee.
4. Divide batter between cake pans and bake until a toothpick inserted in the center comes out clean, 25-30 minutes. Remove cakes from oven, cool for 10 minutes, then move to wire racks.
5. Combine melted chocolate and coconut oil; cool to room temperature. Flip coconut cream can upside down and open from bottom. Discard unsolidified liquid, keeping thick cream at the top. Scoop coconut cream into cold metal bowl. With a handheld mixer, beat coconut cream until fluffy,
6. Slowly drizzle in chocolate, beating until cream gets stiff. Place bowl in refrigerator for 20 minutes.
7. When cakes are cool, place 1 upside down on a plate. Spread a quarter of icing over top, then add second layer on top of icing. Frost top and sides with remaining icing. Top with fresh berries if desired. Cut into 16 slices and serve.

1 SLICE 370 cal., 19g fat (9g sat. fat), 0 chol., 240mg sod., 51g carb. (36g sugars, 3g fiber), 4g pro.

Like Bees to Honey

Mama's azalea bush was the buzz of the neighborhood when a swarm of honeybees paid a visit.

BY CINDY HUDSON

A volleyball-sized swarm of honeybees clung to a branch of Mama's azalea bush in my Louisiana hometown. Four of us watched safely from 10 feet away as the beekeeper, a man of about 75 in jeans, a plaid shirt and work boots, walked up to the branch, grabbed it and gently started to shake it. Thousands of wings beat together in agitation, thrumming a loud warning. Instinctively, the four of us watching stepped back.

I had not lived in this place for nearly 30 years, but I still visited every spring. Mama told me the comings and goings, so I knew we were witnessing the most exciting thing to happen in these parts since lightning struck a telephone pole a year before.

The commotion started the night before when the woman next door knocked on Mama's screen door. "Miss Catherine, are you aware that you have a whole bunch of bees in your azalea bush? I think they're killer bees, and I don't

want them stinging my boys. I've already called the police."

Mama shot out the door and made it halfway across the lawn before I caught up. A few honeybees flew into and out of the perfumed ivory blossoms on Mama's orange trees, flitting around in the golden glow of the sunset. Mama was dismissive.

Above: Cindy and her mom, Catherine, relax together in the yard on a quieter day,

"Where is a swarm, Courtney? I don't see it." Courtney pointed and we followed the flight path of a few bees as they lifted off the flowers and flew toward the azalea bush. Mama gasped out loud.

"You'd better call the exterminator right away," Courtney said. "I don't want my boys to end up in the hospital."

Mama stood with fists balled up at her sides, her lips thinned into a grim line. Living off Social Security and her meager retirement, she counted every penny coming out of her bank account. I knew she was thinking of exterminators, police, screaming children attacked by bees and whether her liability insurance was paid.

Jake, Courtney's dad, who was visiting from down the road, spoke up. "Hold on now. Those are honeybees that broke off from their hive. They do that when they get an extra queen. I bet we could find somebody who wants them."

That somebody ended up being the beekeeper we soon watched at work. He was recruited in the usual way of this small country town: Jake told his neighbor Curt about the swarming bees. Then Curt called his brother-in-law John, who keeps beehives.

When morning came, John and Curt drove up in John's pickup, Jake following behind. There was little in Curt's face I recognized from the days I babysat his two sons, now grown with children of their own. "John is my wife's brother," Curt told me. "His wife died a few months ago."

Already concentrating on the bees, John didn't look up. "Yup, she went home before me," he said. "Now it's just me and the bees. I collect the honey and sell it."

Moving slowly and deliberately, like one of his bees collecting pollen, John grabbed a screened tray with his right hand and continued shaking the azalea branch with his left. Honeybees flew off, swarming his arm and the tray, which he laid on top of the hive he brought with him.

Jake shook his head. "Man, I don't see how you can do that. No suit, no hat, no nothing. Don't you get stung?"

"Nah, you just got to be gentle," John said. "When the bees swarm like this, they're usually gorged with honey. That makes them calm and easy to work around. Later tonight they'll probably be a bit more touchy."

John grabbed a fistful of pine needles, lit them, stuffed them into a smoker and with a bellows puffed smoke at the azalea bush. As he worked, he talked about the way of bees. "The queen is already on the screen; that's why the drones are following her. The smoke will take her scent off the branch, so they won't linger."

In 30 minutes it was all over. John loaded the hive back into his pickup and climbed into the cab. "I'm taking these bees only about a mile down the road," he said. "They'll probably come back for your orange blossoms."

Mama turned toward the back porch and sighed. "Well, I guess that's that. Let's get some lunch."

While eating red beans and rice, we wondered aloud whether the local honey we squeezed on our cornbread came from John's bees. Crickets chirped, mockingbirds sang and the neighborhood settled back to quiet. ♦

Flower Child

··

The blooms beckon on this fourth-generation farm.

BY REBECCA SADLOWSKI

With the seed of caring for nature sown within me, I took root at my family farm at a young age. It was a process to be expected—my roots here go deep, to my great-grandfather Anthony Sadlowski, who bought this 42-acre farm in 1942 with his wife, Julia.

Under my great-grandparents' care, the Sadlowski Farm raised livestock and vegetables, as well as tobacco for a cash crop. Two generations later, my father,

Jeff, still grows tobacco and asparagus through the multigenerational efforts of the whole Sadlowski family. But along with the barns, corncrib and greenhouses that stick out among the tall, broad tobacco leaves and vertical asparagus

··

Above: At Rooted Flower Farm, Rebecca Sadlowski is tied to a sense of community and a connection with nature.

spears, rows and rows of colorful ranunculus and lilac blooms clamor for attention in the springtime, while zinnias and sunflowers get their start nearby.

The Sadlowski Farm—or part of it, anyway—has become Rooted Flower Farm, where we grow floral bouquets and sell them through a Community Supported Agriculture (CSA) model. The roots of this venture also stretch deep.

As a little girl, I couldn't be stopped from running barefoot over to Grammy's and my babci's (great-grandmother's) houses to see what was cooking. I'm rooted to this lifestyle and the sense of community that comes with it.

I'm rooted to the smell of the dirt and the possibility of nature. Some of my earliest memories are of sowing seeds in the greenhouse while my father prepared the garden. It wasn't long after I lost the training wheels on my bike that he started planting corn for my sister and me to pick and sell by the roadside. I tried to convince her that we could use the money to buy more seeds, but she settled with taking the cash instead.

In middle and high school, I carved my own path on the family farm by growing a variety of fresh vegetables. After completing college, my love for growing and selling through my farm stand expanded along with its offerings.

Rooted Flower began as one row of flowers to supplement the vegetables at my stand. One row was followed by two, then three rows and so on over the years as I developed a love for flowers that continues to flourish.

The people visiting our farm stand got my gears turning about flowers. They wanted locally grown blooms, but few knew a farmer who would grow specialty flowers and sell them directly to her customers. (According to industry advocates, nearly 80% of the U.S. flower market is imported, with little attention given to growing practices.)

Driven by my love for the land, I knew I had found my niche. I wanted to support the budding local-flower renaissance by becoming a source in my area for sustainably grown cut flowers. This led to the CSA model, and Rooted Flower Farm was born. I went from growing acres of vegetables to specializing in just under a half-acre of cut flowers.

In our CSA, members pay at the onset of the season for a share of the flowers we will grow. I harvest flowers at their peak time and then carefully select and craft them into beautiful, colorful bouquets that members pick up every week at the farm. Their investment helps to purchase seeds and supplies, repair farm equipment and improve the farm's infrastructure. In return, shareholders receive the freshest blooms possible, many of which are heirloom varieties that, due to their inability to ship well, are not found in stores. My CSA customers also gain an education about what is truly in season for our climate and region.

Rooted Flower Farm is a tribute to those who came before me and those who are with me as I continue to grow. It is my first love. As I harvest this season's beauties, I think about the seed that sprouted in me all those years ago, and I love to share the cuttings from those roots. ◆

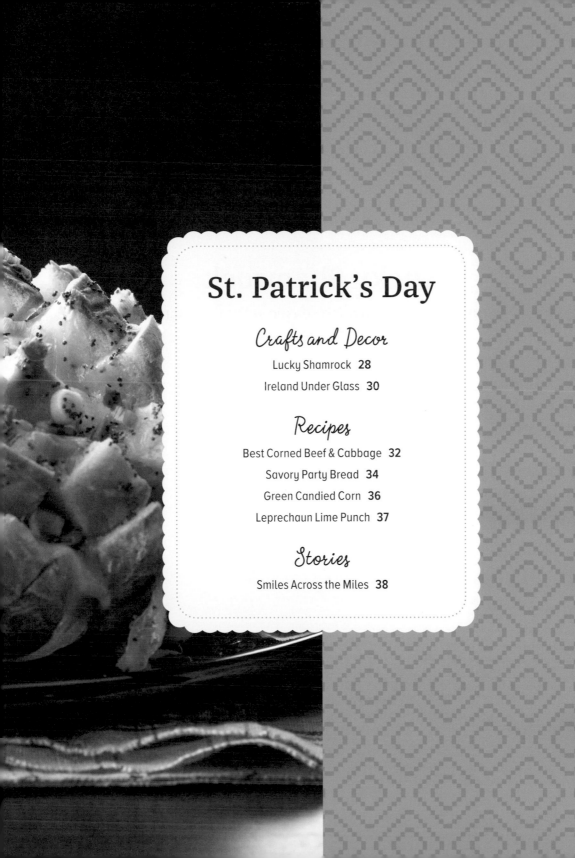

St. Patrick's Day

Lucky Shamrock

Spring-start your growing season with this sprightly little treasure. And make way for rainbows!

WHAT YOU'LL NEED

- Small pot
- Gold spray paint
- Shamrock (oxalis) plant
- Potting soil
- Clover charm
- Green ribbon

DIRECTIONS

1. Spray-paint a small pot gold, applying 2-3 coats and waiting a minute or so between each coat.
2. Plant a lucky shamrock (oxalis) in pot.
3. String a clover charm onto a piece of green ribbon.
4. Wrap ribbon around pot's top edge and tie into a bow.

Ireland Under Glass

Build a mini highland habitat for
some sweet little sheep.

WHAT YOU'LL NEED

- Floral moss variety pack
- Quart mason jar with vintage lid
- 2½-in.-wide roll green sheet moss
- Toothpicks
- Green permanent marker
- Small rocks
- White and black wool roving
- Green paper
- 24-gauge floral wire
- Floral foam scrap piece
- Matte decoupage glue
- Craft paint in 2 shades of brown
- Gardening shears or scissors
- Hot glue gun
- Long tweezers or pliers
- Felting needle
- Felting mat
- Craft knife or cutting machine
- Wire cutters
- Small paintbrush
- Fan paintbrush

DIRECTIONS

1. Place a layer of floral moss in bottom of jar. Cut a circle of sheet moss the diameter of the jar with gardening shears or scissors. Layer on floral moss.

2. Add floral moss to 1 side for hill. Cut a semicircle of sheet moss to cover hill.

3. Cut a few toothpicks into thirds. Discard middle sections. Color points green with a marker. Dry thoroughly.

4. Hot-glue cut end of each toothpick to a rock. Anchor rocks in moss using tweezers.

5. For sheep, start with a cotton ball-sized piece of white wool. Push felting needle about halfway through ball repeatedly, all around, until fibers hold together in an oval about 1 in. long.

6. Repeat with a smaller piece of black wool for the head, working on felting mat if needed.

7. Arrange head on body, and push felting needle into both repeatedly to adhere.

8. Place small amount of black wool on mat to work into ears. Trace a pointed oval shape into wool with needle; fold outer fibers over into oval, pushing them through with needle, to make desired size and shape. Trim any excess.

9. Attach ears to sheep's head, repeatedly pushing needle into head to attach. Fill any indentations in head with black wool.

10. For legs, repeat process but trace a rectangle instead of an oval into the wool before folding

stray fibers over and repeatedly poking them through the mass with needle. Trim with scissors if needed. Attach by poking needle repeatedly through legs and body.

11. For tail, use a tiny piece of white wool; felt it into a ball on mat. Attach to body. Trim stray strands as needed.

12. Make second sheep. Arrange sheep in jar with tweezers.

13. Cut 3- and 4-leaf clovers from paper with craft knife or cutting machine. Place around rocks.

14. Cut fifteen 13-in. pieces of floral wire with wire cutters. Gather and fold in half together. Twist the bunch 3 turns to create 1 in. of twisted wire, leaving a quarter-sized loop at bottom. At the end of the twist, divide wires and twist together to create branches. Continue dividing and twisting until tree is finished. Arrange and trim branches as desired.

15. Cut loop at bottom into 2 or 3 groups of wire. Twist and trim groups for roots, leaving 2 wires pointed

straight down to anchor tree into moss.

16. Anchor tree into floral foam. With paintbrush, apply 2 coats of decoupage glue to tree, filling in spaces between wires. Dry thoroughly between coats, about 4 hours.

17. Paint tree light brown. Dry thoroughly. With a fan brush, lightly apply dark brown paint for bark. Allow to dry thoroughly. Remove tree from floral foam.

18. Stretch floral moss across ends of branches to make leaves. Place tree in jar, using untwisted wires to anchor it in the moss. Arrange branches. Top jar with lid.

Best Corned Beef & Cabbage

It's especially good served with a salad
of peaches and cottage cheese.

—Ruth Warner, Wheat Ridge, Colorado

Prep **10 min.** ◆ Cook **45 min.** ◆ Makes **6 Servings**

WHAT YOU'LL NEED

- **4 cups water**
- **1 corned beef brisket with spice packet (2 pounds)**
- **1 medium head cabbage, cut into 8 wedges**
- **2 large red potatoes, cut into 2-inch chunks**
- **1 can (14 ½ ounces) chicken broth**
- **4 large carrots, cut into 2-inch chunks**
- **1 medium onion, cut into 2-inch pieces**

DIRECTIONS

1. In a 6-qt. electric pressure cooker, combine water and contents of corned beef seasoning packet; add beef. Lock lid; close pressure-release valve. Adjust to pressure-cook on high for 45 minutes.

2. Meanwhile, in a large saucepan, combine the cabbage, potatoes and broth. Bring to a boil. Reduce heat; cover and simmer for 10 minutes. Add carrots and onion. Cover and simmer 20-25 minutes longer or until vegetables are tender; drain.

3. Let pressure release naturally. Remove beef to a serving platter. Discard cooking liquid. Serve beef with cabbage, potatoes, carrots and onion.

1 SERVING 362 cal., 21g fat (7g sat. fat), 105mg chol., 1560mg sod., 22g carb. (9g sugars, 6g fiber), 23g pro.

Savory Party Bread

It's impossible to stop nibbling on warm pieces of this cheesy, onion-y bread.

—Kay Daly, Raleigh, North Carolina

Prep **10 min.** ◆ Bake **25 min.** ◆ Makes **8 Servings**

WHAT YOU'LL NEED

- **1** unsliced round loaf sourdough bread (1 pound)
- **1** pound Monterey Jack cheese
- **½** cup butter, melted
- **½** cup chopped green onions
- **2** to 3 teaspoons poppy seeds

DIRECTIONS

1. Preheat oven to 350°. Cut bread widthwise into 1-in. slices to within ½ in. bottom of loaf. Repeat cuts in opposite direction. Cut cheese into ¼-in. slices; cut slices into small pieces. Place cheese in cuts in bread.

2. In a small bowl, mix butter, green onions and poppy seeds; drizzle over bread. Wrap in foil; place on a baking sheet. Bake 15 minutes. Unwrap; bake until cheese is melted, about 10 minutes longer.

1 SERVING 481 cal., 31g fat (17g sat. fat), 91mg chol., 782mg sod., 32g carb. (1g sugars, 2g fiber), 17g pro.

Tip Make it your own by switching up the cheese (we love smoked Gouda and gooey Brie), customizing seasonings and adding meaty mix-ins. Bacon, diced salami or ham with sliced olives are all terrific choices.

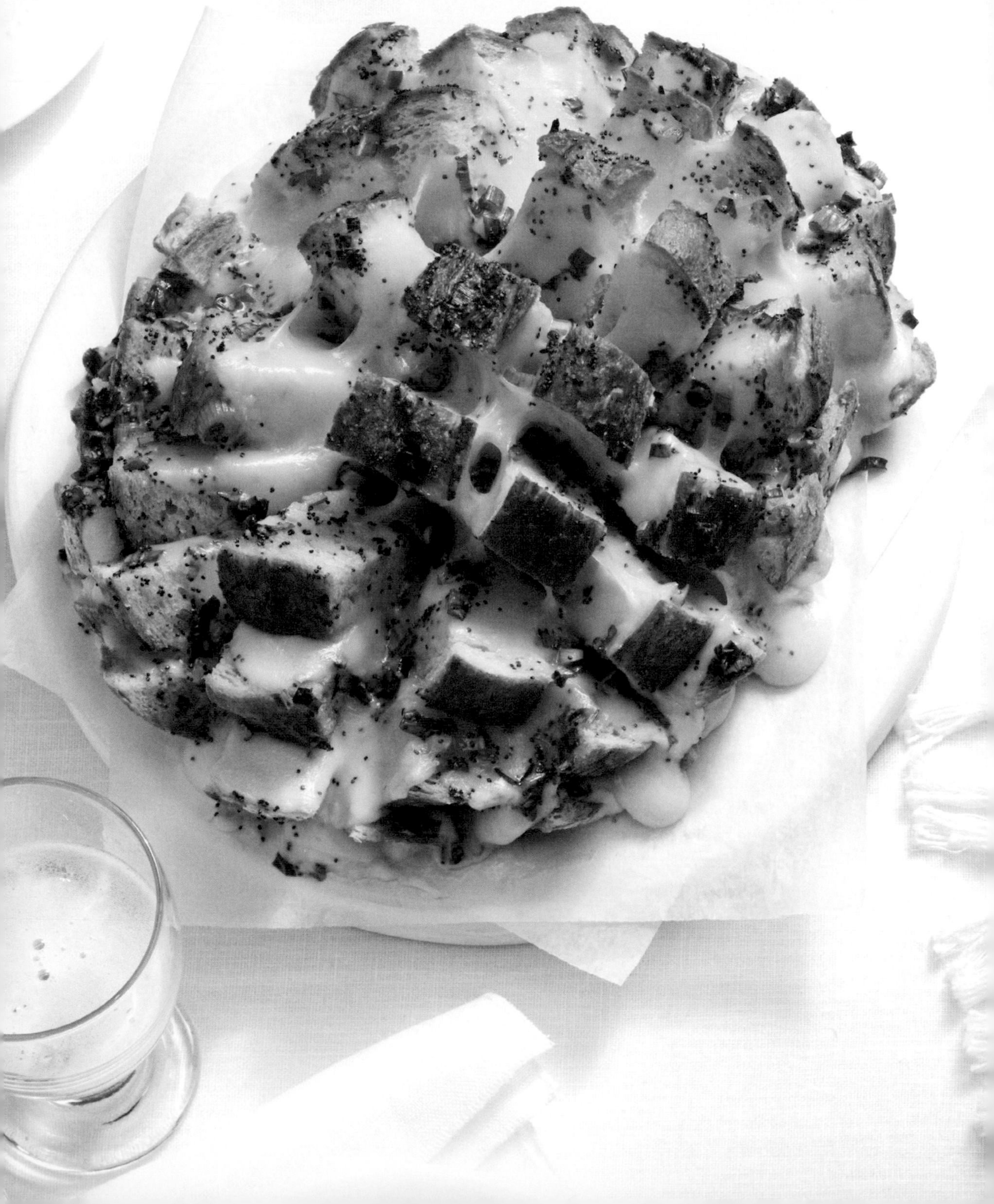

Green Candied Corn

I couldn't stop eating this popcorn when I first
tried it, and now I often take it to gatherings.

—*Courtney Wilson, Fresno, CA*

Prep **30 min.** ◆ Bake **60 min.** ◆ Makes **28 servings (7 quarts)**

WHAT YOU'LL NEED

- 3 packages (3.3 ounces each) butter-flavored microwave popcorn
- 1⅓ cups sugar
- 1 cup light corn syrup
- ½ cup butter, cubed
- 1 teaspoon vanilla extract
- 3 to 5 drops green food coloring, optional

DIRECTIONS

1. Preheat oven to 250°. Pop popcorn according to manufacturer's directions. Transfer to 2 very large bowls; discard any unpopped kernels.
2. In a large heavy saucepan, combine sugar, corn syrup and butter. Bring to a boil over medium heat; cook and stir 3 minutes.
3. Remove from heat; stir in vanilla and, if desired, food coloring. Pour over popcorn and toss to coat. Spread in a single layer on greased 15x10x1-in. baking pans.
4. Bake 1 hour, stirring every 20 minutes. Remove from pans and place on waxed paper to cool. Break into clusters. Store in airtight containers.

1 CUP 151 cal., 6g fat (4g sat. fat), 9mg chol., 125mg sod., 24g carb. (19g sugars, 1g fiber), 1g pro.

Leprechaun Lime Punch

A glass of this marvelous punch in hand is extra lucky indeed.

—Gloria Warczak, Cedarburg, WI

Takes **10 min.** ◆ Makes **20 servings (5 quarts)**

WHAT YOU'LL NEED

- **6** cups refrigerated citrus punch
- **2** cans (12 oz. each) frozen limeade concentrate, thawed
- **¼** cup sugar
- **¼** cup lime juice
- **1** qt. lime sherbet, softened
- **2** liters lemon-lime soda, chilled
- **5** drops green food coloring
  Lime slices

DIRECTIONS

In a large pitcher or punch bowl, combine the citrus punch, limeade, sugar, lime juice and sherbet; stir until smooth and sugar is dissolved. Add soda and food coloring; stir to mix. Float lime slices on top. Serve immediately.

1 CUP 198 cal., 1g fat (0 sat. fat), 0 chol., 41mg sod., 48g carb. (43g sugars, 1g fiber), 0 pro.

Smiles Across the Miles

With a little luck of the Irish, we plant the seeds of gardening love in our grandchildren.

BY GEORGE FLYNN

My wife, Carole, and I love to grow dahlias. Our acreage has many places for us to showcase these carefree, adaptable flowers.

Dahlias flourish in beds, borders and containers. Varying in height and width, they bloom with vibrant hues nonstop from July to frost. Honeybees and butterflies visit them often.

In October, after a cool, sunny stretch of weather, we collect seeds from our favorite plants.

"Jennie will love this color," Carole says as she plucks a dried seed head from a wine-colored Figaro dahlia for our daughter.

Jennie's kids, Miles and Lara, are at ages when they're fascinated by watching new life take root.

Our son Jimmy's kids, Nathan and Noelle, are a little younger but just as eager to sow special seeds from Grandma and Grandpa's gardens.

After plucking one of the dried seedpods, I gently rub it between my fingers, releasing the seeds into a labeled envelope.

We also tag special or sentimental plants whose tubers we'll lift after a killing frost. One gold and red beauty whose petals resemble a tropical sunset was given to Carole by a dear friend who passed away. This is always on her must-save list.

New Jersey winters are cold, snowy and long. But by mid-March, small birds warble at dawn, heralding longer and warmer days ahead. Our thoughts turn back to planting flowers and sharing the seeds we collected in fall.

"The grandkids are just going to love these," Carole predicts as she looks at the smiling leprechauns, Kelly green shamrocks and verses about the luck of the Irish on the cards I picked. In each one she inserts a little glassine envelope containing dahlia seeds chosen especially for that family member.

"Happy St. Patrick's Day, happy spring and happy planting," she writes. "Love, Grandma and Grandpa Flynn."

Timed just right, and with a bit of luck, our mailed cards should arrive on March 17. ♦

Easter

Crafts and Decor

Recipes

Stories

Peep House

Craft a few of these adorable abodes as
a centerpiece for a spring table.

WHAT YOU'LL NEED

- **5 graham cracker squares**
- **Vanilla frosting**
- **1 yellow Peeps candy chick**
- **Green-tinted shredded coconut, jelly beans and pastel sprinkles**

DIRECTIONS

1. Assemble graham cracker squares to resemble a house with 3 walls and a roof. Use frosting to adhere the squares, propping them with small cans until frosting is set.
2. Arrange candy chick on tinted coconut inside house. Decorate house as desired with frosting, jelly beans and pastel sprinkles.

 To tint sweetened shredded coconut, combine 5 drops food coloring per ½ cup coconut in an airtight container; shake until blended.

Twine Eggs

Dress up plastic Easter basket staples with
a cloak of twine.

WHAT YOU'LL NEED

- **5 plastic 2-piece eggs**
- **100 ft. of 2 mm jute twine**
- **Ribbon or lace**
- **Decorative embellishments, such as buttons or beads, optional**
- **Hot glue gun**

DIRECTIONS

1. Separate the eggs into 2 pieces. Beginning at the open end of 1 half, adhere 1 end of the twine with hot glue.
2. Coil the twine around an egg half, adhering with dabs of glue as needed. Continue to the top of the half and cut the twine to fit. Secure with hot glue. Repeat the process with the other egg half.
3. Cut lengths of ribbon or lace to decorate the middle of the eggs. Adhere with glue to only 1 half of each egg at a time so the eggs can be opened to fill with treats.
4. Arrange decorative embellishments, such as buttons or beads, as desired. Secure with hot glue.
5. Repeat process with other 4 eggs.

Blown Eggs

Before you decorate your eggs,
empty them with this simple method.

WHAT YOU'LL NEED

- **Eggs and carton**
- **Large bowl**
- **Thumbtack**
- **Wood skewer**
- **Kitchen or tea towel**
- **Straw cut to 4 in.**

DIRECTIONS

1. With egg in carton, press thumbtack firmly into the top and bottom of egg to puncture shell.
2. At the bottom of the egg, insert the sharp end of a skewer and rotate it to break up the yolk. Wrap the egg in a towel and shake it several times to further break up the contents.
3. Place a straw over the hole at the top of the egg and blow out contents into a bowl. If yolk does not flow easily out of the egg, repeat steps 2 and 3 as needed until egg is empty. Discard the egg contents or reserve for another use.
4. Wash egg in warm, soapy water; dry. Blow through egg a final time to ensure that the inside of the shell is completely clear.

NOTE There is no limit to the ways you can decorate blown eggs. You can paint them, glue on feathers or beads or any other embellishments you like, or decoupage them with washi paper (see page 48).

Washi Paper Eggs

Skip the messy dyes and style eggs with colorful washi paper to create a cheerful Easter decoration.

WHAT YOU'LL NEED

- **Blown Eggs (see page 46)**
- **Washi or origami paper in various colors**
- **Measuring tape**
- **Ruler**
- Cutting mat
- Craft knife
- Decoupage glue
- Paintbrush

DIRECTIONS

1. Start with an empty egg shell.
2. Cut washi paper ⅛ in. bigger than circumference and height of the egg.
3. Fold paper in half lengthwise, then again crosswise.
4. Cut ¼-in. strips along the long side of the paper, stopping ¼ in. before the center fold.
5. Trim the ends of each ¼-in. strip to a point. Unfold paper and place wrong side up on a piece of parchment paper.
6. Use a brush to spread on a thin layer of glue.
7. Lay egg against a short side and wrap paper around the egg. Press each strip toward the tip of the egg, 1 piece at a time. Each strip should slightly overlap the previous strip. Work your way slowly around the egg, smoothing out the paper strips with your fingers. Brush glue over the top of each strip of paper as you go. Repeat on bottom half of egg.
8. Apply a layer of glue over the entire egg, and set on parchment paper to dry.

Pack the Perfect Basket

Treat every member of the family
to an Easter surprise designed just for them.

1. A BAKER'S DOZEN

For that person whose happiest moments are spent blending butter and flour, pack baking tools, gadgets, and a cookbook or two into a pretty mixing bowl, canister or cookie jar. Think about those tools you're always reaching for: hot pads, dish towels and spatulas. Add a favorite ingredient, a go-to cake mix or a fancy bottle of vanilla extract. Arrange it in the container and tuck in a handwritten recipe card.

2. CRAFT A CREATIVE'S DREAM

If a sis scrapbooks and an auntie crochets, a trip to the craft store is in order to pick up skeins of yarn, needles, pretty papers, rolls of washi tape, calligraphy pens, decorative scissors, fat quarters, thread or maybe a fancy new glue gun with some glitter glue sticks. Consider a few crafty items for hobbies they haven't yet taken up—maybe a book on creating paper flowers or a pattern for a simple embroidery design. Creative types are always looking for new outlets for their passions. Organize the surprises in a practical basket that will keep everything neat in a workroom.

3. GIFTS FOR GREEN THUMBS

For the gardener on your list, opt for a few classics—think bulbs and seeds—along with a few unexpected gardening gadgets, like a good pair of pruners, a pair of gloves with sturdy grips or a new hose nozzle. A traditional basket is perfect to pack it all in because the person can use it later to gather flowers or fruit from garden beds. But if your gardener works more in containers, look for a new terra-cotta pot to fill with green-thumb fun.

4. DON'T FORGET FIDO

Let the Easter Bunny pamper the pooch, too, with a new doggie dish full of his favorite things. Nothing says "pet-friendly" better than a bag of homemade treats, a new squeaky toy, a fashionable collar and a brush to keep his locks tangle-free. Put the edibles (and chewables) into a new food bowl, and then see how many sloppy dog kisses you get when he finds his "basket."

5. EASTER, DELIVERED

When Raeann Thompson's son, Sgt. Anthony Miles, was deployed overseas during the 2017 Easter season, she made sure the Easter Bunny delivered his basket from her Wisconsin home via the U.S. Postal Service. After filling a shipping box with chocolate eggs and other goodies, she decorated the inside edges of the box with a spring motif so he'd get an extra surprise as soon as he opened the package. If your box is going overseas, Raeann suggests making a full inventory of the contents before heading to the post office—the customs form for international mail requires a detailed list.

6. SPA DAY FOR MOM

Give Mom a basket that promises rest and relaxation. Gather bath salts and fancy soaps, a fragrant candle, a soft sleep mask, a tin of good tea, a fluffy robe, and maybe a book to get lost in or a journal to jot down inspirations. Package these luxuries in a pretty basket that matches Mom's bathroom decor—not only will it look great for gift-giving, but later it can become a catchall on her vanity.

Crab Deviled Eggs

My family loves crab salad and deviled eggs, so I tried combining the two. The crabmeat adds a lot of flavor. What a hit!

—Kevon Shuler, Chelsea, MI

Takes **30 min.** ◆ Makes **2 dozen**

WHAT YOU'LL NEED

- 12 hard-boiled large eggs
- 1 can (6 oz.) crabmeat, drained, flaked and cartilage removed
- ½ cup mayonnaise
- 1 green onion, finely chopped
- 1 Tbsp. finely chopped celery
- 1 Tbsp. finely chopped green pepper
- 2 tsp. Dijon mustard
- 1 tsp. minced fresh parsley
- ½ tsp. salt
- ⅛ tsp. pepper
- 3 dashes hot pepper sauce
- 3 dashes Worcestershire sauce
  Additional minced fresh parsley, optional

DIRECTIONS

1. Cut eggs lengthwise in half. Remove yolks, reserving whites. In a bowl, mash yolks. Stir in next 11 ingredients.
2. Spoon or pipe into egg whites. Refrigerate, covered, until serving. If desired, sprinkle with fresh parsley.

1 STUFFED EGG HALF 76 cal., 6g fat (1g sat. fat), 100mg chol., 160mg sod., 0 carb. (0 sugars, 0 fiber), 4g pro.

Spinach Chicken Salad

Dazzle hungry visitors with this crunchy salad. The delectable dressing complements the colorful ingredients.

—Janet Mooberry, Peoria, IL

Prep **20 min. + chilling** ♦ Makes **10 servings**

WHAT YOU'LL NEED

- 5 cups cubed cooked chicken (about 3 whole breasts)
- 2 cups green grape halves
- 1 cup snow peas
- 2 cups packed torn spinach
- 2½ cups sliced celery
- 7 oz. spiral pasta or elbow macaroni, cooked and drained
- 1 jar (6 oz.) marinated artichoke hearts, drained and quartered
- ½ large cucumber, sliced
- 3 green onions with tops, sliced

DRESSING

- ½ cup canola oil
- ¼ cup sugar
- 2 Tbsp. white wine vinegar
- 1 tsp. salt
- ½ tsp. dried minced onion
- 1 tsp. lemon juice
- 2 Tbsp. minced fresh parsley
- Optional: Large spinach leaves and orange slices

DIRECTIONS

1. In a large bowl, combine the chicken, grapes, peas, spinach, celery, pasta, artichoke hearts, cucumber and green onions. Cover and refrigerate. In a small bowl, whisk 7 dressing ingredients. Cover and refrigerate.
2. Just before serving, whisk dressing and pour over salad; toss to coat. If desired, serve on spinach leaves and garnish with oranges.

1 CUP 313 cal., 16g fat (2g sat. fat), 54mg chol., 396mg sod., 21g carb. (12g sugars, 3g fiber), 22g pro.

Horseradish-Glazed Ham

This glaze is our favorite way to perk up a baked ham. The leftovers make zippy sandwiches—with more horseradish, of course.

—Cathy & Monte Seus, Tulelake, CA

Prep **15 min.** ◆ Bake **1 hour 40 min.** ◆ Makes **12 servings**

WHAT YOU'LL NEED

- **1** fully cooked bone-in ham (5 to 6 lbs.)
  Whole cloves
- **1** cup packed brown sugar
- **⅓** cup prepared horseradish
- **¼** cup lemon juice

DIRECTIONS

1. Using a sharp knife, score surface of ham with ¼-in.-deep cuts in a diamond pattern; insert a clove in each diamond. Bake according to package directions.
2. Meanwhile, mix remaining ingredients. Brush over ham during the last 30 minutes of baking.

4 OZ. COOKED HAM 232 cal., 5g fat (2g sat. fat), 83mg chol., 1026mg sod., 20g carb. (19g sugars, 0 fiber), 28g pro.

Traditional Hot Cross Buns

On Easter morning, our family always looked forward to a breakfast of dyed hard-boiled eggs and Mom's hot cross buns.

—Barbara Jean Lull, Fullerton, CA

Prep **25 min.** + rising ◆ Bake **15 min.** ◆ Makes **2½ dozen**

WHAT YOU'LL NEED

- 2 pkg. (¼ oz. each) active dry yeast
- 2 cups warm whole milk (110° to 115°)
- 2 large eggs, room temperature
- ⅓ cup butter, softened
- ¼ cup sugar
- 1½ tsp. salt
- 1 tsp. ground cinnamon
- ¼ tsp. ground allspice
- 6 to 7 cups all-purpose flour
- ½ cup dried currants
- ½ cup raisins
- 1 large egg yolk
- 2 Tbsp. water

ICING

- 1½ cups confectioners' sugar
- 4 to 6 tsp. whole milk

DIRECTIONS

1. In a small bowl, dissolve yeast in warm milk. In a large bowl, combine eggs, butter, sugar, salt, spices, yeast mixture and 3 cups flour; beat on medium speed until smooth. Stir in currants, raisins and enough remaining flour to form a soft dough (dough will be sticky).

2. Turn onto a floured surface; knead until dough is smooth and elastic, 6-8 minutes. Place in a greased bowl, turning once to grease the top. Cover and let rise in a warm place until doubled, about 1 hour.

3. Punch down dough. Turn onto a lightly floured surface; divide and shape into 30 balls. Place 2 in. apart on greased baking sheets. Cover with kitchen towels; let rise in a warm place until doubled, 30-45 minutes. Preheat oven to 375°.

4. Using a sharp knife, cut a cross on top of each bun. In a small bowl, whisk egg yolk and water; brush over tops. Bake for 15-20 minutes or until golden brown. Remove from pans to wire racks to cool slightly.

5. For icing, in a small bowl, mix confectioners' sugar and enough milk to reach desired consistency. Pipe a cross on top of each bun. Serve warm.

1 BUN 171 cal., 3g fat (2g sat. fat), 28mg chol., 145mg sod., 31g carb. (12g sugars, 1g fiber), 4g pro.

Fluffy Bunnies

Whip a cup of mousse or pudding into a
sweet Easter surprise—just add edible ears!

—Matthew Mead, Concord, NH

Takes **5 min.** ◆ Makes **1 serving**

WHAT YOU'LL NEED

Pastel miniature
marshmallow
Parfait glass
6 pieces uncooked
angel hair pasta (2 in. each)
Prepared mousse
or pudding
1 palmier cookie
White sprinkles, optional

DIRECTIONS

1. For bunny nose, cut marshmallow in half. Press cut edge of 1 half against the side of the parfait glass until the marshmallow sticks.

2. For whiskers, gently insert 1 end of each pasta piece into the marshmallow, placing 3 whiskers on each side of nose.

3. Fill the parfait glass with prepared mousse or pudding and insert palmier, positioning cookie so that it resembles bunny ears. Top with sprinkles if desired. Serve immediately.

NOTE We used Jell-O brand butterscotch pudding to fill in this recipe, but you can use whatever brand or flavor you prefer.

½ **CUP PUDDING WITH 1 PALMIER** 245 cal., 8g fat (5g sat. fat), 10mg chol., 285mg sod., 41g carb. (25g sugars, 2g fiber), 1g pro.

 Tip Surround glass with an extra scoop of marshmallows for the taking.

Love in a Paper Bag

This Easter custom will endure for generations.

BY ANDREW RICCHIUTI

When my mother, Catherine, spoke of grandchildren and customs, she always said, "Be careful of what you start, because then you have to continue."

She was probably thinking about Easter bags.

It began the first Easter after the birth of my oldest son, her first grandchild. He was about 5 months old and way too young for an Easter basket full of jelly beans, chocolate and other sugary candies. Instead, she bought food, clothing, diapers and other items that we needed for the baby.

When she spread out all the booty on the floor, it wouldn't fit into one Easter basket. She had to use a brown paper bag from the local supermarket.

But there was a problem: The bag didn't look anything like an Easter basket. Sure, it held many items, but it looked as if she'd just come back from grocery shopping. Where was the Easter theme?

She turned to my father for help since he could draw. He drew Easter characters on the bag, and they both filled them in with bright colors. Covered in decorations, the bag looked like an Easter basket.

This tradition continued through nine grandchildren. For almost 20 years after my father, Andrew, died, Mom made the bags herself. Each grandchild received one until the age of 12. Then, after 12, he or she usually got an Easter card with a little cash.

Far left: Owen, Avery and Evan get Easter bags, thanks to their Great-Grandma Catherine (right, with baby Natalia).

Those grandchildren now range in age from 12 to 40 years old, and some still have their last Easter bag. When my wife and I had our first grandchild in 2008, we revived the tradition. To date, we have six grandchildren, and Mom lived to meet all of them.

Truthfully, neither my wife nor I can draw, so we glue clip art we find online or window decals to the bags. We shop for what the kids like and for what the parents will approve. The bags overflow with goodies, toys and books.

The biggest problem in this age of plastic bags is finding paper bags without any lettering on them. It takes time and patience, but we manage to do it.

Our grandchildren anticipate diving into their bags. They love them so much that we've started a similar tradition for Halloween.

As Mom said, we should have been careful of what we started. ♦

Scrambling for Eggs

An Easter fiasco sends the adults on the hunt.

BY DARIS HOWARD

One Easter weekend, my in-laws, John and Corky, planned a big egg hunt at my daughter's house.

They bought 96 plastic eggs and lots of candy to fill them. John and I would hide the eggs, and then my younger children and grandchildren would hunt for them.

"You think you can find some good hiding places?" John asked.

"Not only can I find some great places to hide the eggs," I joked, "but with my memory, I'll never be able to find them all."

He laughed, "If there's candy in them, the children will find them."

The next morning, we were still asleep when the grandchildren pounced on us. "Is it time to hunt for Easter eggs, Grandpa?" my granddaughter asked.

I knew I wasn't going to get any more sleep, so I got up and cooked breakfast. Afterwards, it was all we could do to keep them inside while John and I hid the eggs.

We worked hard to find the best spots, and it took about 20 minutes to hide them all. We'd just finished and told the children they could hunt when Corky appeared with a big bag of candy.

"John," she asked, "have you seen the plastic eggs that I bought? I can't find them."

He glanced at me and turned to Corky, "You didn't fill them?"

"No," she replied. "I was just getting ready to."

My grandson came over to show me a plastic egg he found. I opened it and, sure enough, it was empty. We collected the ones the children had found and shooed them back inside so that John and I could try to find the rest. When we finished, we could only find 82.

John grinned at me. "I guess you were right: We could hide our own Easter eggs and never find them."

Corky filled the ones we found, and John and I hid them again. We kept a bag of candy with us, and when the children found one of the empty rogue eggs, we magically filled it for them. But then they realized that if they emptied the full ones and brought them back to us, we'd fill those, too. Pretty soon our candy bag was empty. We hadn't planned to give them all the candy; it just worked out that way. My little granddaughter climbed on my lap and said, "Grandpa, I'm glad you're forgetful."

I smiled and hugged her. I guess every cloud has a silver lining. ♦

Itty-Bitty Easter Biddies

A father's simple surprise leaves
a lasting memory for his children.

BY NELDA HOWELL LOCKAMY

I t was the early 1950s, and yet another hard-candy Christmas had come and gone in our little pocket of the Blue Ridge Mountains. Little was expected and little was received in terms of bicycles or Betsy Wetsy dolls. While the six of us kids questioned the existence of a Santa Claus who would leave such meager fare under our scrawny tree, we were in for a more memorable holiday at Easter thanks to my father.

Some three weeks before Easter, our father had set one of his fat Dominique hens on a clutch of eggs. We kids did not have access to the chicken house during this time, and if indeed the eggs hatched before Easter morning, it was a closely guarded secret.

As soon as it became daylight, Daddy emerged from the henhouse carrying his everyday hat, an old engineer's cap from his railroading days. As he rounded the path by the spring, we could hear faint peeps. Daddy bent down on the porch and presented the cap's treasure to his children. Inside was a pile of quivering, pale yellow biddies—one for each of us. While Mother watched this presentation with

....

Holding those chicks reinforced the meaning of Easter for Nelda.

the awe it deserved, Daddy's calloused hands cupped each chick. Repeating the admonition to handle them gently, he placed a trembling fluff of flesh into each pair of outstretched hands.

The chicks were barely dry, smelled of the barnyard and had chips of eggshell matted to their feathers. But to a 6-year-old they felt like pulsating gold, their cottony feathers and parchment skin stretched over tiny bones. We children cuddled the chicks until Daddy declared that their clucking mother missed them. After we had given each of them a name (mine was Goldilocks) and were convinced that we could positively identify our own, we placed the wobbly peeps back in Daddy's cap so that he could return them to their nervous mother's nest.

I don't recall playing with the Easter hatchlings again, nor did we get too excited over future broods that spring. At some level, we must have connected them to the chicken and dumplings that showed up at every Sunday dinner. But that simple Easter surprise was our sunrise service and Alleluia chorus all rolled into a single event. When the miracle of new life had caused tears to roll down my father's face, there was no room to doubt the message we heard in church that day. ♦

Mother's Day

Crafts and Decor

Recipes

Stories

Seed Packet Wreath

Make planting time even more enjoyable with this beautiful decoration.

WHAT YOU'LL NEED

- **Seed packets for bird-, bee- or butterfly-friendly plants**
- **Grapevine wreath**
- **String**
- **Card stock**
- **Corrugated cardboard**
- **Decorative scrapbook paper**
- **Wire**
- **Decorative ribbon**
- **Dried seedpods or flowers**
- **Hole punch**
- **Craft knife**
- **Craft glue**
- **Hot glue gun**
- **Wire cutters**
- **Needle-nose pliers**

DIRECTIONS

1. Punch a hole in corner of each seed packet and tie to wreath with string.
2. On card stock, print "For the Birds," "For the Butterflies" and "For the Bees" tags. Cut out, punch holes and tie them to appropriate seed packets.
3. Copy the template for the butterfly, bee and bird shapes (see page 214) on card stock. Cut out and trace onto the corrugated cardboard. Cut shapes with craft knife. Scale templates a little smaller; print on card stock. Cut out and trace onto cardboard. Cut shapes with craft knife. Repeat process at least once more.
4. Stack the cutouts to create a 3D effect and glue together with craft glue. Embellish shapes with decorative scrapbook paper. (Use the inner layers of the templates as guides). Hot-glue shapes to wreath.
5. Cut lengths of wire and twist into antennae shapes with pliers. Insert antennae wires into open cells of cardboard edges, securing with glue.
6. Tie a bow with decorative ribbon and secure to wreath with length of wire. Hot-glue seedpods and other embellishments onto wreath.

Cast-Iron
Scrambled Eggs

I love these easy cast-iron scrambled eggs that use fresh
ingredients I usually have on hand. They make
a quick and simple breakfast!

—Bonnie Hawkins, Elkhorn, WI

Takes **25 min.** ◆ Makes **6 servings**

WHAT YOU'LL NEED
- 12 **large eggs**
- 2 **Tbsp. water**
- ¼ **tsp. salt**
- ¼ **tsp. pepper**
- ⅔ **cup finely chopped sweet onion**
- 1 **jalapeno pepper, seeded and chopped**
- 2 **Tbsp. butter**
- 1 **log (4 oz.) fresh goat cheese, crumbled**
- 3 **Tbsp. minced chives**

DIRECTIONS
1. In a large bowl, whisk the eggs, water, salt and pepper; set aside.
2. Place a 10-in. cast-iron skillet over medium-high heat. In the skillet, saute onion and jalapeno in butter until tender. Add egg mixture; cook and stir until almost set. Stir in cheese and chives; cook and stir until eggs are completely set.

⅔ **CUP** 217 cal., 16g fat (7g sat. fat), 446mg chol., 342mg sod., 3g carb. (2g sugars, 0 fiber), 15g pro.

Mom's Chocolate Bread

My mom made this divine chocolaty bread for holidays or at special request. I always think of my family when I smell it baking.

—*Rachel Rhodes, Princeton, NC*

Prep **10 min.** ◆ Bake **30 min. + cooling** ◆ Makes **1 loaf (12 slices)**

WHAT YOU'LL NEED

- 4 Tbsp. sugar, divided
- 3 Tbsp. all-purpose flour
- 1 Tbsp. cold butter
- 1 to 3 Tbsp. ground cinnamon
- 1 tube (8 oz.) refrigerated crescent rolls
- ⅔ cup semisweet chocolate chips
- 1 Tbsp. butter, melted

DIRECTIONS

1. Preheat oven to 375°. For streusel, in a small bowl, mix 3 Tbsp. sugar and flour; cut in butter until crumbly. Reserve half the streusel for topping. Stir cinnamon and remaining sugar into remaining streusel.

2. Unroll crescent dough into a long rectangle; press perforations to seal. Sprinkle with chocolate chips and cinnamon mixture. Roll up jelly-roll style, starting with a long side; pinch seam to seal. Fold roll in half lengthwise; transfer to a greased 8x4-in. loaf pan. Brush with butter; sprinkle with reserved streusel.

3. Bake until golden brown, 30-35 minutes. Cool in pan 10 minutes before removing to a wire rack to cool completely.

1 SLICE 164 cal., 9g fat (4g sat. fat), 5mg chol., 165mg sod., 21g carb. (11g sugars, 2g fiber), 2g pro.

Spumoni Baked Alaska

For a dazzling yet refreshing end to a meal, try this freezer finale.

—Taste of Home *Test Kitchen*

Prep **50 min. + freezing** ◆ Bake **5 min.** ◆ Makes **12 servings**

WHAT YOU'LL NEED

- ½ cup butter, cubed
- 2 oz. unsweetened chocolate, chopped
- 1 cup sugar
- 1 tsp. vanilla extract
- 2 large eggs, room temperature
- ¾ cup all-purpose flour
- ½ tsp. baking powder
- ½ tsp. salt
- 1 cup chopped hazelnuts
- 2 qt. vanilla ice cream, softened, divided
- ½ cup chopped pistachios
- ½ tsp. almond extract
- 6 drops green food coloring, optional
- ⅓ cup chopped maraschino cherries
- 1 Tbsp. maraschino cherry juice
- 1 Tbsp. rum

MERINGUE
- 8 large egg whites, room temperature
- 1 cup sugar
- 1 tsp. cream of tartar

DIRECTIONS

1. Preheat oven to 350°. In a microwave-safe bowl, melt butter and chocolate; stir until smooth. Stir in sugar and vanilla. Add eggs, 1 at a time, beating well after each addition. Combine flour, baking powder and salt; gradually stir into chocolate mixture. Stir in hazelnuts.

2. Spread into a greased 8-in. round baking pan. Bake until a toothpick inserted in the center comes out with moist crumbs (do not overbake), 35-40 minutes. Cool 10 minutes before removing from pan to a wire rack to cool completely.

3. Meanwhile, line an 8-in. round bowl (1½ qt.) with foil. In a smaller bowl, place 1 qt. ice cream; add pistachios, almond extract and, if desired, food coloring. Quickly spread ice cream over bottom and up sides of foil-lined bowl, leaving center hollow; cover and freeze for 30 minutes.

4. In a small bowl, combine cherries, cherry juice, rum and remaining 1 qt. ice cream. Pack ice cream into hollow center of 8-in. bowl; cover and freeze.

5. In a large heavy saucepan, combine egg whites, sugar and cream of tartar. With a hand mixer, beat on low speed 1 minute. Continue beating over low heat until egg mixture reaches 160°, about 8 minutes. Transfer to a bowl; beat until stiff glossy peaks form and sugar is dissolved.

6. Place brownie on an ungreased foil-lined baking sheet; top with inverted ice cream mold. Remove foil. Immediately spread meringue over ice cream, sealing to edges of brownie. Freeze until ready to serve, up to 24 hours.

7. Preheat oven to 400°. Bake until the meringue is lightly browned, 2-5 minutes. Transfer to a serving plate; serve immediately.

1 PIECE 554 cal., 29g fat (13g sat. fat), 94mg chol., 314mg sod., 68g carb. (52g sugars, 3g fiber), 11g pro.

Easy Fresh Strawberry Pie

I often use whole fresh strawberries and arrange them pointed side up in the pastry shell for a different presentation.

—Josh Carter, Birmingham, AL

Prep **20 min.** + cooling ◆ Bake **15 min.** + chilling ◆ Makes **8 servings**

WHAT YOU'LL NEED

- 1 sheet refrigerated pie crust
- ¾ cup sugar
- 2 Tbsp. cornstarch
- 1 cup water
- 1 pkg. (3 oz.) strawberry gelatin
- 4 cups sliced fresh strawberries
  Whipped cream, optional

DIRECTIONS

1. Preheat oven to 450°. Unroll crust into a 9-in. pie plate. Trim edge. Line unpricked crust with a double thickness of heavy-duty foil or parchment. Bake 8 minutes. Remove foil; bake 5 minutes longer. Cool on a wire rack.

2. In a small saucepan, combine sugar, cornstarch and water until smooth. Bring to a boil; cook and stir until thickened, about 2 minutes. Remove from the heat; stir in gelatin until dissolved. Refrigerate until slightly cooled, 15-20 minutes.

3. Meanwhile, arrange strawberries in the crust. Pour gelatin mixture over berries. Refrigerate until set. If desired, serve with whipped cream.

1 PIECE 264 cal., 7g fat (3g sat. fat), 5mg chol., 125mg sod., 49g carb. (32g sugars, 2g fiber), 2g pro.

A Treasured Recipe

....

If company was coming, Mom made a batch of her
no-bake cookies—whether we wanted them or not!

.... BY JACQUIE McTAGGART ....

My mother's recipe box contains a free trip down memory lane, an excursion my family and I can repeat at will.

I discovered this on a cool, crisp autumn day as I searched through my own recipe box for a knock-your-socks-off soup that would kick off the fall season in style. I found several contenders, but none of them made my mouth water.

And then I remembered: The chicken noodle soup made by my mother, Maybelle Bowers, was to die for. All I had to do was find her recipe box. I raced to the cedar chest, pushed aside a few family mementos and pulled out Mom's 4-by-5-inch tin recipe box—the one with the little red hearts stenciled on the sides.

The box, which had sat in the chest untouched for the three years since Mom's passing, served as an apparition. I could see my mother's shape, hear her soft laughter and feel her gentle touch in my mind. I imagined her putting the little tin box in my hand, the two of us sitting on the sofa together to begin our jaunt down memory lane.

Mom's recipe box, unlike my own, had no category dividers. Consequently, her Best Ever Mint Dessert from a woman named Blondie was tucked haphazardly between Toby's Peach Pie and a Salmon Puff recipe with no attribution.

Merry Dee's Carrot Glaze took me back 70 years, to the phone call when Mom learned her sister, brother-in-law and two nephews had been killed in an automobile accident. Mom's niece Merry was the only survivor.

My mind flooded with pleasant memories when I came to Aunt Elsie's Chicken Rice Casserole. Although not a blood relative, Aunt Elsie was an aunt in our hearts. She and Mom played together as toddlers and kept up their strong friendship for a remarkable 94 years. As with all best friends, they celebrated life's happy events together and supported each other through the rougher patches. And, judging from Mom's tin box, they shared a lot of recipes.

As it turned out, there was no recipe for chicken noodle soup in Mom's box.

Apparently that was one of her "a little of this and a little of that" recipes that never got written down. And my very favorite memory trigger, a recipe for boiled cookies, can't be found in Mom's box either. Protected in a plexiglass frame, this treasure rests at the top left corner of my refrigerator door, next to Mom's last church directory picture and a gold angel magnet.

My mother's only culinary clunker—in my opinion—were no-bake, boiled cookies. They are incredibly simple to make and, admittedly, beloved by many families. Just not ours.

Mother discovered this recipe shortly after she and Dad moved from Iowa to Florida in the fall of 1967. That Christmas my husband, two young sons and I traveled to Bonita Springs to celebrate with Grandma and Grandpa. After we all arrived, Mom went to the kitchen and returned with a heaping plate of chocolate no-bake cookies.

I found them too sweet, too chocolaty and too lumpy, but not wanting to hurt her feelings, I pretended to like them.

Big mistake. For the next 45 years, Mom's "company's coming" prep always included a double batch of no-bake cookies—right up to the day she passed away.

On Feb. 5, 2012, my husband and I were headed westward to spend a week with Mom, who, by then, was 97 and in

relatively good health in Mesa, Arizona. My phone rang. It was my sister.

"Jacquie," she said, "are you in heavy traffic right now?"

She didn't have to say anything more. I knew. Mom was gone.

Later, as the details of Mom's last morning unraveled, I smiled. She had worn her Ultrasuede pantsuit to breakfast at her assisted living residence and visited with fellow residents.

About 20 minutes after she left the dining room, a nurse stopped by her apartment to administer the morning meds. She found Mom on the floor of her kitchenette, along with a generous amount of what the paramedics termed "chocolate pudding." The oats, sugar and cocoa sat on the counter—next to a recipe card for her no-bake boiled cookies.

I am confident Mom's final morning was a joyful one. She looked forward to our visit and was happy to make her special company's coming treats.

I'll probably never make a batch of Mom's cookies, but I'll treasure that recipe card on the fridge forever. ♦

Maybelle Bowers' recipe box holds many memories of family and friends for daughter Jacquie McTaggart.

Chocolate Oat Boiled Cookies

These peanut butter and chocolate cookies bring back fond memories of my mom. The no-bake recipe was her favorite.

—Jacquie McTaggart, Independence, IA

Prep **20 min.** + **chilling** ◆ Makes **2½ dozen**

WHAT YOU'LL NEED

- **2 cups sugar**
- **½ cup butter or margarine, cubed**
- **½ cup 2% milk**
- **3 Tbsp. baking cocoa**
  Dash salt
- **½ cup creamy peanut butter**
- **1 tsp. vanilla extract**
- **3 cups old-fashioned oats**

DIRECTIONS

1. In a large saucepan, combine first 5 ingredients. Bring to a boil, stirring constantly. Cook and stir 3 minutes.

2. Remove from heat; stir in peanut butter and vanilla until blended. Stir in oats. Drop mixture by tablespoonfuls onto waxed paper-lined baking sheets. Refrigerate until set. Store in airtight containers.

1 COOKIE 139 cal., 6g fat (3g sat. fat), 8mg chol., 50mg sod., 20g carb. (14g sugars, 1g fiber), 2g pro.

Mother-Daughter Farming

Quality time, country-style.

BY BRANDEE MOORE

The day our 250-pound calf escaped was terrifying, hilarious and annoying all at once. It started when my daughter, Shelby, and I were driving the gravel road between two of our pastures and came upon the rogue calf outside the barbed wire fence. I instructed Shelby to let me out at the gate, ease the truck past and around him, and then flush him back toward me. I'd open the gate and boom! No need to call my father for backup.

As Shelby pulled away to get ahead of the calf, he sped up. I made some major arm motions, signaling her to go faster!

Our crazy llama (left) created a whole lot of chaos—and a funny bonding moment—for my daughter, Shelby, and me. Shelby and I work with calves and steers at rodeos, as well as at home on the farm. Life is good when gates are shut! At right, we're about to work with a new set of cows and babies.

She gunned it, shot past the calf and did a half U-turn in the gravel road, cutting him off. Whew, one step of our plan was complete.

As I hustled to open the gate, I saw Crazy Llama coming my way. (We have two llamas on our farm; one is pleasant and one is not. The one heading my way was the unpleasant one.) He stayed on his side of the fence but seemed utterly fascinated by my hair. My dad always told me never to show fear, because animals can sense it. I'll tell you, it's really hard to remain calm when a llama is reaching over a fence and diving at your head.

At this point, Shelby was down the road, doubled over laughing, as I ducked to escape Crazy Llama's advances. Still, I got the gate open. Keep in mind, it's not some fancy-schmancy gate that might swing easily. Nope, this one is basically a hog panel, albeit a deluxe hog panel, that must be lifted up a bit to fit and then kept in place with some spare wire.

By some miracle I lured Crazy Llama down the fence away from the opening, and Shelby nudged the calf toward it. He was in! Just then Crazy Llama dived for the calf and the gate panel fell over—apparently the llama had been standing close enough to prop up the panel when the wire that usually kept it in place broke moments earlier.

While I hurried to raise the gate and shut it, the commotion got Crazy Llama's attention and he turned back! We closed the panel before he came after us. But then came the chore of rewiring everything while he ran back and forth the length of it, trying to decide whether to nail Shelby or me. If someone had

taken a video of us, we would have been winners of something.

As we walked to the truck, my dad pulled up and asked what we were doing. When we told him, he said, "Oh, that calf is always out. He does that when I leave the gate open to feed, but he always finds his way back in."

So, folks, remember that open gates lead to way more trouble than they're worth. Always shut them behind you, and make sure your gates are sturdy. You never know when a crazy llama will be waiting. ♦

Father's Day

Crafts and Decor

Recipes

Stories

Tie Wreath

Celebrate a well-dressed loved one by turning their old ties into a wreath that's knotted in style.

WHAT YOU'LL NEED

- **14-18 neckties**
- **14-in. foam wreath form**
- **Flat-head straight pins**
- **Card stock**
- **Coordinating heavy-duty thread**
- **Three ¾-in. buttons, as desired**
- **20-gauge wire**
- **Fabric glue**
- **Wire cutters**
- **Sewing needle**

DIRECTIONS

1. Arrange ties to find a pleasing color scheme. Cut the wide ends of neckties to 14-15 in. long.
2. Pin cut end of necktie at back of wreath near the outside edge. Wrap around wreath until point of necktie is in position with point facing out. Pin in place. Continue pinning and wrapping neckties until wreath base is covered.
3. On card stock, draw a template, similar to a baseball diamond, that fits into the end of a tie. Cut same number of shapes as ties used. Remove pin holding point of first tie in place. Insert card into back of tie point, trimming as necessary for individual ties, and glue in place with fabric glue. Repeat process for all ties.
4. Glue back of tie to wreath with permanent fabric glue to secure.
5. To make flowers, cut 14-in.-long pieces from discarded ends of ties. Tie a knot close to cut end of each piece. Stitch a running stitch along 1 long end of tie. Pull thread tightly to gather into a rosette. Secure with a few stitches at back. Sew button in center of rosette. Repeat with 2 ties.
6. Arrange rosettes, and pin securely or glue to wreath.
7. Cut a 6-in. length of wire and bend into a loop. Twist cut ends tightly and insert into back of wreath, between ties, to form a hanger. Secure with glue if needed.

Country-Style Grilled Ribs

A sweet and tangy barbecue sauce coats these tender ribs. Chili powder and hot pepper sauce contribute to the zesty flavor.

—Marilyn Beerman, Worthington, OH

Prep **1½ hours + standing** ◆ Grill **10 min.** ◆ Makes **6 servings**

WHAT YOU'LL NEED

- **4 lbs.** bone-in country-style pork ribs
- **1 cup** water
- **1 cup** ketchup
- **¼ cup** packed brown sugar
- **¼ cup** cider vinegar
- **¼ cup** Worcestershire sauce
- **1 Tbsp.** celery seed
- **1 tsp.** chili powder
- **⅛ tsp.** hot pepper sauce
- Dash pepper

DIRECTIONS

1. Preheat oven to 325°. Place ribs in a shallow roasting pan. Bake, covered, 1½-2 hours or until meat is tender. Meanwhile, in a small saucepan, combine the remaining ingredients. Bring to a boil. Reduce heat; simmer, uncovered, 5 minutes, stirring occasionally. Pour 1 cup sauce over ribs; turn to coat. Let stand 15 minutes.
2. Drain and discard sauce from ribs. Grill ribs, uncovered, over medium heat 10-12 minutes or until browned, basting with 1 cup sauce and turning occasionally. Serve with remaining sauce.

1 SERVING 409 cal., 18g fat (7g sat. fat), 114mg chol., 463mg sod., 24g carb. (23g sugars, 0 fiber), 35g pro.

Backyard Red Potato Salad

Here's a potato salad that has no mayo, so it's perfect for outdoor picnics. Plus, it looks just as good as it tastes.

—*Holly Bauer, West Bend, WI*

Prep **25 min.** ◆ Grill **10 min.** ◆ Makes **9 servings**

WHAT YOU'LL NEED

2½ lbs. small red potatoes
1 medium onion,
   cut into ½-in. slices
½ cup olive oil, divided
1 tsp. salt, divided
½ tsp. pepper, divided
3 Tbsp. balsamic vinegar
2 Tbsp. lemon juice
1 Tbsp. Dijon mustard
2 tsp. sugar
2 garlic cloves, minced
¼ cup minced
   fresh tarragon

DIRECTIONS

1. Place potatoes in a large saucepan; cover with water. Bring to a boil. Reduce heat; cover and cook 10 minutes. Drain; cool slightly. Cut each in half.

2. In a large bowl, combine the potatoes, onion, ¼ cup oil, ½ tsp. salt and ¼ tsp. pepper; toss to coat. Arrange vegetables, cut side down, on a grilling grid; place on a grill rack. Grill, covered, over medium heat for 8-10 minutes or until vegetables are tender and lightly browned, turning occasionally. Chop onion. Place onion and potatoes in bowl.

3. In a small bowl, whisk the vinegar, lemon juice, mustard, sugar, garlic and the remaining oil, salt and pepper. Add to potato mixture; toss to coat. Sprinkle with tarragon. Serve warm or at room temperature. Refrigerate leftovers.

¾ **CUP** 215 cal., 12g fat (2g sat. fat), 0 chol., 312mg sod., 24g carb. (4g sugars, 3g fiber), 3g pro. **DIABETIC EXCHANGES** 2 fat, 1½ starch.

Sweet & Smoky Salsa

I love the roasted flavor that comes from grilling,
so I decided to make a salsa with grilled vegetables.

—Shelly Bevington, Hermiston, OR

Prep **1 hour** ◆ Process **15 min.** ◆ Makes **4 pints**

WHAT YOU'LL NEED

- **1** cup soaked mesquite wood chips
- **2** medium onions
- **12** garlic cloves, peeled
- **3** tsp. barbecue seasoning, divided
- **2** lbs. tomatillos, husked (about 12)
- **2** lbs. plum tomatoes (about 8)
- **6** jalapeno peppers
- **1½** cups cider vinegar
- **1¼** cups packed brown sugar
- **1½** tsp. salt
- **½** tsp. pepper
- **⅓** cup minced fresh cilantro

DIRECTIONS

1. Add mesquite wood chips to grill according to manufacturer's directions.
2. Cut onions in quarters; place in a small bowl. Add garlic and 1½ tsp. barbecue seasoning; toss to coat. Grill, covered, over medium heat for 10-15 minutes or until tender, turning occasionally.
3. Meanwhile, cut tomatillos, tomatoes and jalapenos in half; place in a large bowl. Add remaining barbecue seasoning; toss to coat. Grill in batches, covered, over medium heat 4-6 minutes or until tender, turning occasionally.
4. Chop vegetables. Transfer to a Dutch oven; stir in vinegar, brown sugar, salt and pepper. Bring to a boil. Reduce heat; simmer, uncovered, 15-20 minutes or until slightly thickened. Stir in cilantro.
5. Carefully ladle hot mixture into 4 hot 1-pint jars, leaving ½-in. headspace. Remove air bubbles and adjust headspace, if necessary, by adding hot mixture. Wipe rims. Center lids on jars; screw on bands until fingertip tight.
6. Place jars into canner with simmering water, ensuring that they are completely covered with water. Bring to a boil; process for 15 minutes. Remove jars and cool.

¼ **CUP** 49 cal., 0 fat (0 sat. fat), 0 chol., 180mg sod., 11g carb. (9g sugars, 1g fiber), 1g pro. **DIABETIC EXCHANGES** ½ starch.

Bacon Chocolate Chip Cheesecake Blondies

There's nothing better than a cookie, brownie and cheesecake mixed together, with bacon to top it off!

—*Katie O'Keeffe, Derry, NH*

Prep **30 min.** ◆ Bake **45 min.** + chilling ◆ Makes **16 servings**

WHAT YOU'LL NEED

- 8 bacon strips, cooked and crumbled
- 1 cup butter, softened
- ¾ cup sugar
- ¾ cup packed brown sugar
- 2 large eggs, room temperature
- 1 tsp. vanilla extract
- 2¼ cups all-purpose flour
- 1 tsp. salt
- 1 tsp. baking soda
- 2 cups semisweet chocolate chips

CHEESECAKE LAYER

- 2 pkg. (8 oz. each) cream cheese, softened
- 1 cup sugar
- 2 large eggs
- ¾ cup 2% milk
- 2 tsp. vanilla extract

DIRECTIONS

1. Preheat oven to 375°. Line a 9-in. square baking pan with foil, letting ends extend up sides; grease the foil.

2. Reserve ¼ cup crumbled bacon for top. In a large bowl, cream butter and sugars until light and fluffy, 5-7 minutes. Beat in eggs and vanilla. In another bowl, whisk flour, salt and baking soda; gradually beat into creamed mixture. Stir in chocolate chips and remaining bacon. Press half the dough onto bottom of prepared pan.

3. For cheesecake layer, in a large bowl, beat the cream cheese and sugar until smooth. Add eggs, milk and vanilla; beat on low speed just until blended. Pour over dough in prepared pan; drop remaining dough by rounded tablespoonfuls over cheesecake layer. Sprinkle with reserved bacon.

4. Bake until golden brown, 45-50 minutes. Cool in pan on a wire rack. Refrigerate at least 4 hours before cutting. Lifting with foil, remove from pan. Cut into bars.

1 BAR 534 cal., 31g fat (18g sat. fat), 113mg chol., 523mg sod., 61g carb. (45g sugars, 2g fiber), 8g pro.

The Good Guys Always Win

When the insurance man came calling, Pawpaw schooled him in old-fashioned common sense.

BY TONY BURTON

Pawpaw trudged up the path from the cow barn, a bucket in each hand. I ran alongside, trying to keep up. He slowed his pace. "I'm tired so I think I'll walk a mite slower," he said.

"I'll carry the milk if you want me to," I offered. He just smiled, shaking his head.

Pawpaw placed the milk in the old refrigerator to cool and washed his hands. He entered the living room and sat down with a sigh. I followed, a 4-foot-tall shadow.

"Is it time for wrestling yet?" I asked.

"Almost," he said. "About 10 minutes." He laid his head on the back of his chair and closed his eyes.

The quiet in the house was intense. Mawmaw was visiting Aunt Eunice, so the usual sound of her singing was absent.

Footsteps on the walk outside upset the quiet. A man in a dark suit and straw hat stood at the screen door. He peered in through the wire mesh, rapping on the door frame. "Anybody home?" he said.

Pawpaw opened one eye reluctantly, then the other. With a sigh, he heaved himself up and went to unlatch the door.

"Come in, Mr. Allen," he said, standing aside as the man entered. "Have a seat. Anthony and I were about to watch wrestling, if you'd care to join us."

The man shook his head. "No, Arthur, I'm afraid I don't have time. I came by to see if you'd changed your mind about that insurance policy. It's very important to protect your loved ones, you know."

Pawpaw looked at the man. "I reckon I keep 'em pretty safe, Mr. Allen."

I piped up. "Pawpaw wouldn't let nothing hurt me!"

The man threw a pained smile my way. "Arthur, I mean after you're dead and gone, and you know that. I understand you take care of your family now, but who will provide for them when you die?" He had a sort of whiny, wheedling voice, similar to how old Mrs. Parsons sounded when she was trying to get her billy goat back in the pen.

He removed a folded piece of limp pink paper from his jacket pocket. "This policy will cost you only one dollar each week, and after it has been in force for three months, if you die, Continental Life will pay your wife $1,000!" He extended the paper toward Pawpaw, who was looking at his watch. It was time for wrestling, and he was missing the introduction of the Masked Avenger and his opponent, the evil Baron von Smelt.

Pawpaw shook his head. "Mr. Allen, insurance don't make sense to me." He leaned forward, his hands splayed out on his knees. "I pay you a dollar each week?"

Mr. Allen nodded, pleased. "That's right! A pittance."

"Uh-huh. And your company will pay Beulah $1,000 if I die?"

Mr. Allen raised a warning hand. "If you die after the policy has been in force for three months."

Pawpaw nodded. "Now, if I do my sums correctly, and I cross over Jordan after three months, I'll have paid you about $14, and you'll pay Beulah $1,000."

The man nodded again.

"But," Pawpaw continued, "if I keep living for a few years, say five more, I'll pay you more than $250."

Mr. Allen looked wary, "Yes, but..."

Pawpaw continued over the objection: "And saying the good Lord lets me live 20 more years, that means I'll have paid your company over $1,000. That right?"

"I...I believe you are correct, yes," the man stammered.

"So, for me to come out ahead on this deal, I have to die pretty soon. And for you to get ahead, I have to live to a ripe old age," Pawpaw shook his head. "The way I see it, you're betting I'll live a long time, and I'm betting that I won't."

He got up, still shaking his head, and went to open the screen door. Mr. Allen followed. "I'm not a betting man, Mr. Allen," Pawpaw said. "And if I was, I sure wouldn't go betting against myself."

Pawpaw placed a hand gently but firmly on the man's back and guided him out the door. "Thanks for stopping by, but I don't need insurance."

We sat down, I in Pawpaw's lap. His arm wrapped around me protectively. On TV, the Masked Avenger had Baron von Smelt pinned to the canvas. I nodded. The good guy always wins! ♦

Never Too Old for Home

....

Every time we cast a line, Daddy and I catch
memories that are bigger than any fish in the lake.

.... BY AMIE ROLLAND ....

A dad is every child's hero—if they're lucky enough, as I am, to have a great one. I'm an English teacher in Beijing, China, who was born and raised in north Louisiana. After I moved away, my folks sold our home and bought a new place on the lake.

I was a bit leery of returning to this new house, but when I walked in, it was home. Family photos line the hallways and shelves. My dad's drums sit in a room full of Dallas Cowboys memorabilia and enough records and CDs to open a music store.

My favorite thing about going home is fishing with Daddy. When I was home recently, it rained most of the time, but as long as the rain wasn't accompanied by thunder and lightning, my dad was standing in the backyard throwing a line.

When he isn't working, you can find him fishing. While growing up, I took our time fishing together for granted—if I'm not hooking anything, I get bored. I realize now how precious our time together is. Whenever I fish with Daddy, I think about Trace Adkins' song "Just Fishin'"; it is always more than that.

Eternity wouldn't be enough time to go fishing with my dad. Living abroad has taught me to cherish the smallest of moments. But we shouldn't have to be separated to remember how much our family loves us.

Though they live in different parts of the world, Amie always makes time for her dad.

We never talk about the really personal things, because I'm his girl and he's my daddy, ya know? But the thing I love most about my dad is how he reacted when he knew I was unhappy in our hometown. I'll never forget the moment he told me I should leave home.

That was painful for him, I know. And I see how it takes every ounce of his courage and strength to put me on a plane each time I leave. I can never thank him enough for giving me the push I needed.

I take after my dad in many ways, and I'm thankful for each of those traits, even the bad habits. I love the bond we share, and although I can't remember every moment, I have millions stored away.

I'm writing this to ask you all to remember and cherish your family every day, not just on the holidays. Happy Father's Day, Dad. I promise to never get so wrapped up in this crazy life that I forget how to find my way home. ♦

Summer

Crafts and Decor

Recipes

Stories

Frilly Flower Vase

Dress up jars with hand-me-down doilies
for a lacy new look.

WHAT YOU'LL NEED

- **Mason jars or vases**
- **Doilies or lace**
- **Decorative ribbon or twine**
- **Spray adhesive**

DIRECTIONS

1. Thoroughly clean jar or vase inside and out. Let dry.
2. Measure doily or lace to cover the exterior of the jar. Trim if needed.
3. Place doily right side down on work surface. Spray the opposite side with adhesive.
4. Apply doily to mason jar, smoothing out wrinkles as much as possible.
5. Decorate with ribbon, raffia or twine.

Personalized Walking Stick

Rack up miles and memories with this walking stick.
Oh, the places you'll go!

WHAT YOU'LL NEED

- 2-3 sturdy sticks
- Paracord
  (nylon parachute cord)
- Sandpaper
- Spray paint
- Glue gun
- Waxed paper
- Paintbrush
- Polyurethane clear gloss

DIRECTIONS

1. Strip the bark from the sticks. If the sticks are damp, allow them to dry indoors for several days. Sand them smooth.
2. Cover work surface with newspaper in a well-ventilated area. Lay out sticks and spray-paint top sides. Let dry. Turn over sticks and spray-paint the other sides until they are fully coated. If sticks need multiple coats, repeat spray-painting, letting paint dry for a minute or so between applications.
3. For handle, wrap the top of each stick with paracord. Glue the ends of cord to secure.
4. Download a digital image of each desired park emblem. Size the images to fit your walking sticks and flip them so they will print in reverse.
5. Cut an 8½x11-in. rectangle from waxed paper. Load printer with 1 waxed paper sheet and print an emblem. Allow ink to set for 1 minute, then carefully lay printed image over stick and press the wet ink onto it, exerting even pressure for a good transfer. Remove waxed paper. Repeat with remaining emblems.
6. Use a brush to paint walking sticks with clear gloss.

 Tip Choose sticks that have a 1-2-in. diameter. Trim them to a comfortable height for walking.

Watermelon Wreath

A bright slice of hello offers a fresh and fun welcome.

WHAT YOU'LL NEED

- **1 yard of fabric in each color: green, light pink, dark pink**
- **Wire wreath form**

- Black buttons
- Needle
- Black thread

DIRECTIONS

1. Start with 1 yard of fabric in each color. Cut 1-inch by 7-inch strips.
2. Tie green strips of fabric around the outer rim of the wire wreath form.
3. Tie light pink strips of fabric on the next ring of the form.
4. Tie strips of dark pink fabric on the two innermost rings.
5. Fluff the strips, and sew shiny black button "seeds" on several dark pink pieces.

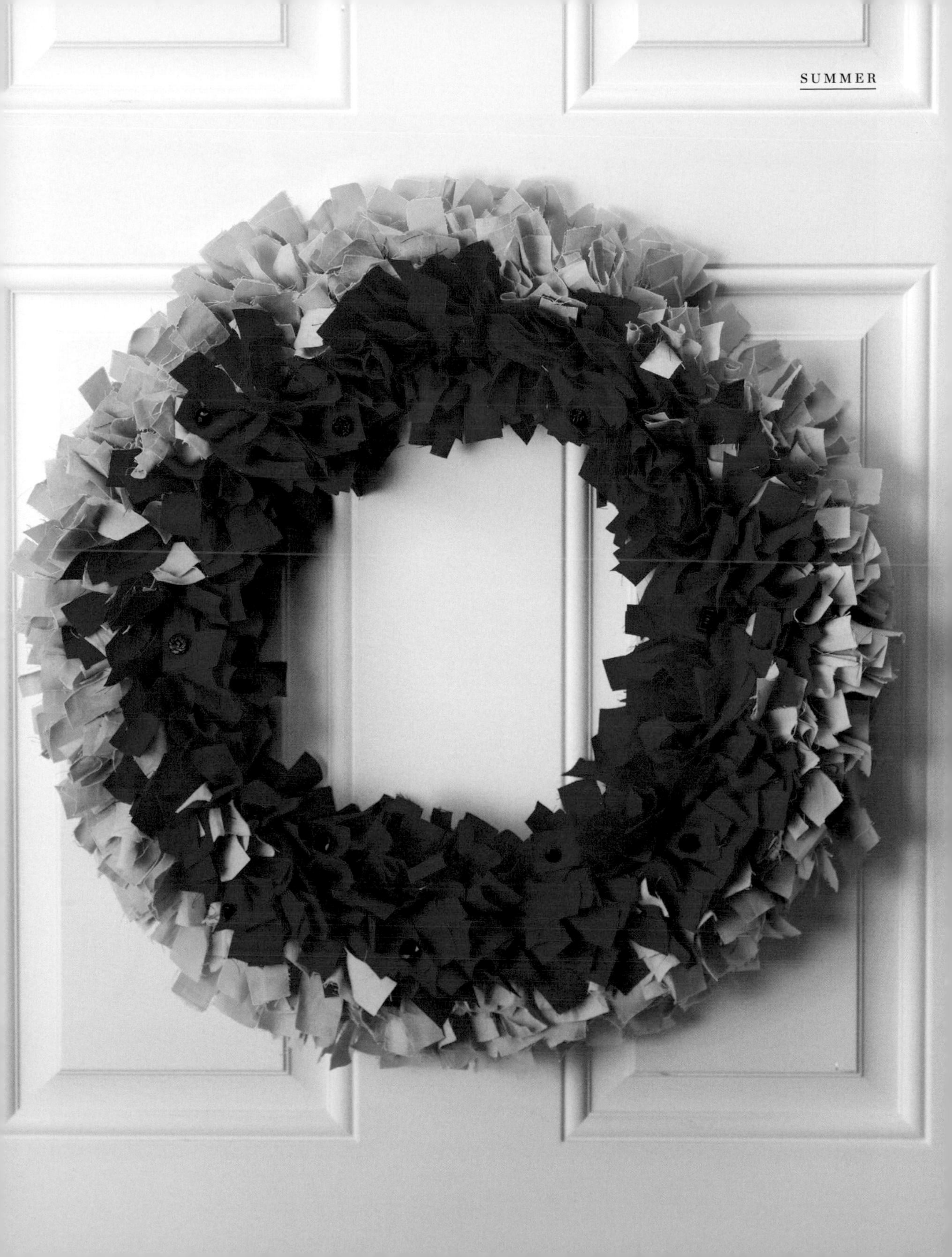

Making It Their Own

A pair of DIYers repurposed family heirlooms
to decorate their cozy cabin home.

Melissa and Wade Yocum dreamed of building their home in Northumberland, Pennsylvania, on 11 acres they inherited from Wade's grandparents.

With a plan in place in 2011, they began construction of a log home within walking distance of where Wade grew up. "Our home project was 90% self-build because we wanted to save money and were capable of doing a lot of the work ourselves," Melissa says. "But we ran into many obstacles along the way."

A flood that year delayed the basement excavation, and then the company from which they purchased the log home kit went out of business. They finally moved in during the summer of 2013. "It was not completely finished, but it was done enough to live in!" Melissa says.

She set to combing antique and thrift stores for pieces to repurpose into furniture and fixtures for their new home. "We wanted our home to have a unique, cozy cabin feel, so we chose items that were rustic with lots of patina. Looking back, it was a lot of fun to find things for our home—much like a treasure hunt," Melissa says. "But it also took a lot of patience and work to get the items made into things that were usable."

1. FAMILY HEIRLOOMS

Wade crafted the Yocum's dining room table and benches from a tree that fell on their property. He created a light fixture out of a sign that once hung in his uncle's garage.

2. A SHOWER CURTAIN WITH HISTORY

In the 1980s, Melissa's mom embroidered a set of hankies that Melissa's great-grandmother had sewn. Melissa arranged those around a Pennsylvania-themed one she found and sewed them into a shower curtain. "It warms my heart to be able to look at it every day," she says.

3. ON THE LEVEL

A sliding door leads to the master bath and a walk-in closet. "We used metal roofing to make it look like a barn," Melissa says. An old level became a handy row of hooks on the door.

4. WASH DAY FUN

Melissa uses an old galvanized basin as a sink in her combined laundry and bathroom. A metal horse hame—a section of harness—attached to the wall serves as a towel bar. Vintage enamel lights, advertising signs and soda crates complete the look. And a metal cabinet makes space for the family to display its extensive magnet collection. "There are many items in our home that have stories, either about the people who gave them to us or how we acquired them, says Melissa.

5. KID-FRIENDLY CREATIONS

A few years ago, Melissa and Wade adopted two children, and since then they've focused on creating functional pieces for the kids to use. Here, Melissa turned a small stepladder into a handy bookcase.

Grilled Shrimp Salad with Coconut Vinaigrette

The secret to this refreshing combination is the coconut-milk marinade—it makes the shrimp incredibly tender and flavorful.

—Sarah Vasques, Milford, NH

Prep **20 min.** + marinating ◆ Grill **10 min.** ◆ Makes **4 servings**

WHAT YOU'LL NEED

- **1** cup coconut milk
- **⅓** cup honey
- **2** Tbsp. rice vinegar
- **1** Tbsp. canola oil
- **¼** tsp. salt
- **1** lb. uncooked shrimp (26-30 per pound), peeled and deveined

SALAD

- **4** cups spring mix salad greens
- **1** cup green grapes
- **½** cup sweetened shredded coconut
- **½** cup dried cranberries
- **¼** cup sliced almonds, toasted

DIRECTIONS

1. In a small bowl, combine the first 5 ingredients. Pour ¾ cup into a shallow dish. Add the shrimp; turn to coat. Cover and refrigerate for up to 30 minutes. Cover and refrigerate remaining vinaigrette.

2. Drain and discard vinaigrette from shrimp. Thread shrimp onto 4 metal or soaked wooden skewers.

3. Grill shrimp on an oiled rack, covered, over medium heat or broil 4 in. from the heat until shrimp turn pink, turning once, 6-8 minutes. Divide salad ingredients among 4 plates; top with shrimp. Serve with reserved vinaigrette.

1 SALAD 425 cal., 19g fat (12g sat. fat), 138mg chol., 283mg sod., 46g carb. (37g sugars, 4g fiber), 22g pro.

Grilled Red Pepper Dip

We grill peppers with rosemary and garlic, then blend them with sun-dried tomatoes for a creamy spread to pass with pita chips.

—Donna Alwine, Bloomington, IN

Prep **20 min.** + cooling ◆ Grill **5 min.** ◆ Makes **4¾ cups**

WHAT YOU'LL NEED

- 2 large sweet red peppers, halved and seeded
- 1 Tbsp. olive oil
- 1 tsp. garlic powder
- 1 tsp. minced fresh rosemary
- 2 pkg. (8 oz. each) cream cheese, softened
- ⅔ cup finely chopped oil-packed sun-dried tomatoes
- 2 garlic cloves, minced
- 1 tsp. onion salt
- 2 cups crumbled feta cheese
- Pita chips

DIRECTIONS

1. Toss peppers with oil, garlic powder and rosemary to coat. Grill peppers, covered, over medium-high heat or broil 4 in. from heat 2-3 minutes on each side or until tender. Cool completely. Cut peppers into ¼-in. pieces.
2. In a large bowl, beat cream cheese, sun-dried tomatoes, garlic and onion salt until blended. Beat in feta cheese and chopped red peppers until blended. Serve with pita chips. Refrigerate any leftover dip.

¼ **CUP** 127 cal., 11g fat (6g sat. fat), 29mg chol., 280mg sod., 4g carb. (2g sugars, 1g fiber), 4g pro.

Lemon Basil Salmon

My husband came up with this easy, foil-packet recipe for flaky, fork-tender salmon. This one is a winner.

—Marianne Bauman, Modesto, CA

Takes **20 min.** ◆ Makes **2 servings**

WHAT YOU'LL NEED
- **2 salmon fillets (5 oz. each)**
- **1 Tbsp. butter, melted**
- **1 Tbsp. minced fresh basil**
- **1 Tbsp. lemon juice**
- **⅛ tsp. salt**
- **⅛ tsp. pepper**
- **Lemon wedges, optional**

DIRECTIONS
1. Prepare campfire or grill for medium heat. Place each fillet, skin side down, on a piece of heavy-duty foil (about 12 in. square). Mix melted butter, basil, lemon juice, salt and pepper; spoon over salmon. Fold foil around fish, sealing tightly.
2. Cook on campfire or in covered grill until fish just begins to flake easily with a fork, 10-15 minutes. Open foil carefully to allow steam to escape. If desired, serve with lemon wedges.

1 FILLET 274 cal., 19g fat (6g sat. fat), 86mg chol., 264mg sod., 1g carb. (0 sugars, 0 fiber), 24g pro.
DIABETIC EXCHANGES 4 lean meat, 1½ fat.

Fruit & Almond Bites

With big handfuls of dried apricots, cherries, almonds and pistachios, these are some seriously satisfying no-bake treats.

—Donna Pochoday-Stelmach, Morristown, NJ

Prep **40 min. + chilling** ◆ Makes **about 4 dozen**

WHAT YOU'LL NEED

- 3¾ cups sliced almonds, divided
- ¼ tsp. almond extract
- ¼ cup honey
- 2 cups finely chopped dried apricots
- 1 cup finely chopped dried cherries or cranberries
- 1 cup finely chopped pistachios, toasted

DIRECTIONS

1. Place 1¼ cups almonds in a food processor; pulse until finely chopped. Remove almonds to a shallow bowl; reserve for coating.
2. Add remaining 2½ cups almonds to food processor; pulse until finely chopped. Add extract. While processing, gradually add honey. Remove to a large bowl; stir in apricots and cherries. Divide mixture into 6 portions; shape each into a ½-in.-thick roll. Wrap and refrigerate until firm, about 1 hour .
3. Unwrap and cut rolls into 1½-in. pieces. Roll half the pieces in reserved almonds, pressing gently to adhere. Roll remaining half in pistachios. If desired, wrap individually in waxed paper, twisting ends to close. Store in airtight containers, layered between waxed paper if unwrapped.

1 PIECE 86 cal., 5g fat (0 sat. fat), 0 chol., 15mg sod., 10g carb. (7g sugars, 2g fiber), 2g pro. **DIABETIC EXCHANGES** 1 fat, ½ starch.

Sugar Cookie Tarts

Whenever we visit family in Maryland, everybody offers ways to improve recipes. That's how this dessert came to be.

—Barb White, Ligonier, PA

Takes **20 min.** ◆ Makes **4 servings**

WHAT YOU'LL NEED

- **1 tsp. cornstarch**
- **3 Tbsp. water**
- **2 Tbsp. orange juice**
- **1 Tbsp. lemon juice**
- **Dash salt**
- **5 Tbsp. sugar, divided**
- **3 oz. cream cheese, softened**
- **4 large sugar cookies (3 in.)**
- **Assorted fresh fruit**

DIRECTIONS

1. For glaze, in a small saucepan, mix first 5 ingredients until smooth; stir in 3 Tbsp. sugar. Bring to a boil over medium heat; cook and stir until thickened, 1-2 minutes. Cool slightly.

2. In a small bowl, mix cream cheese and remaining sugar until smooth; spread over cookies. Top with fruit. Gently brush with glaze. Refrigerate until serving.

1 TART 189 cal., 9g fat (5g sat. fat), 26mg chol., 463mg sod., 25g carb. (21g sugars, 0 fiber), 2g pro.

 Tip Sugar cookies from the bakery make a speedy crust.

Down East Blueberry Buckle

This buckle won a contest at my daughter's college. They shipped us four lobsters, but the real prize was seeing the smile on our daughter's face.

—Dianne van der Veen, Plymouth, MA

Prep **15 min.** ◆ Bake **30 min.** ◆ Makes **9 servings**

WHAT YOU'LL NEED

- 2 **cups all-purpose flour**
- ¾ **cup sugar**
- 2½ **tsp. baking powder**
- ¼ **tsp. salt**
- 1 **large egg,**
  room temperature
- ¾ **cup 2% milk**
- ¼ **cup butter, melted**
- 2 **cups fresh or frozen**
  blueberries

TOPPING

- ½ **cup sugar**
- ⅓ **cup all-purpose flour**
- ½ **tsp. ground cinnamon**
- ¼ **cup butter, softened**

DIRECTIONS

1. Preheat oven to 375°. In a large bowl, whisk flour, sugar, baking powder and salt. In another bowl, whisk egg, milk and melted butter until blended. Add to flour mixture; stir just until moistened. Fold in blueberries. Transfer to a greased 9-in. square baking pan.

2. For topping, in a small bowl, mix sugar, flour and cinnamon. Using a fork, stir in softened butter until mixture is crumbly. Sprinkle over batter.

3. Bake until a toothpick inserted in center comes out clean, 30-35 minutes (do not overbake). Cool in pan on a wire rack. Serve warm or at room temperature.

1 PIECE 354 cal., 12g fat (7g sat. fat), 49mg chol., 277mg sod., 59g carb. (32g sugars, 2g fiber), 5g pro.

Help from the Hoosier

Each year as the summer kitchen hummed with activity, turning seasonal produce into winter sustenance, a handy cupboard held it all together.

BY JANIS PARR

Until I got married and moved from the city to the country, I had never heard of a summer kitchen or a "Hoosier." But as a new farm wife, I quickly learned that almost every old farmhouse—including the one I had just moved into—had a summer kitchen with a Hoosier cabinet, in addition to the larger kitchen inside the house.

Those summer kitchens were treasured by their owners. They usually housed a sink, a stove, a table and chairs, and a Hoosier—a multipurpose cabinet often referred to as a mother's helper.

Mine was indeed a help. Hoosiers contain shelves and drawers with pullout cutting boards made of wood, porcelain or enamel. They have spice racks and cookbook crannies, and many have built-in bread boxes and sugar and flour bins, complete with sifters. A summer kitchen rarely had any other cupboards or counters, so the mother's helper was a blessing.

The summer kitchen always had more than one door and several windows through which the fresh cool breezes could blow on a warm summer day. My summer kitchen had three windows and four doors. During canning season, the cool air was most welcome as I stood at the stove, making jam and sterilizing jars. Baskets of fresh strawberries, blueberries and peaches would be lined up on the

sturdy old chrome table, waiting to be made into delicious jams and pies.

The mother's helper stood by with everything I needed to make pastry for my made-from-scratch pies. Crocks of pickles had their place on the old table, each crock waiting for the next step in the pickle-making process. I still remember the delicious smell of spices when I'd make the syrup for those pickles—a tantalizing blend of sugar, vinegar, cinnamon and pickling spice that the neighbors could smell all the way down the road, or so they said. Somehow the summer kitchen managed to hold on to those spicy smells no matter the time of year.

Remembering my summer kitchen from so many years ago, along with all the delicious things that came from that busy little space to nurture my family, brings fond memories I will treasure always. Even though I no longer live in the country or have a summer kitchen, I still have my mother's helper. It is nearly 80 years old now and is the same one my mother-in-law used and loved for so many years as well. ♦

Janis Parr still has her mother-in-law's Hoosier cabinet.

Best Ever Sweet Pickles

I grow cucumbers on our urban backyard trellis to make these.

—Ellie Martin Cliffe, Milwaukee, WI

Prep **1 hour + standing**   ◆   Process **10 min.**   ◆   Makes **4 pints**

WHAT YOU'LL NEED

- **9** cups sliced pickling cucumbers
- **1** large sweet onion, halved and thinly sliced
- **¼** cup canning salt
- **1** cup sugar
- **1** cup water
- **1** cup white vinegar
- **½** cup cider vinegar
- **2** Tbsp. mustard seed
- **1** tsp. celery seed
- **½** tsp. whole peppercorns
- **12** garlic cloves, crushed
- **4** bay leaves

DIRECTIONS

1. In a large nonreactive bowl, combine cucumbers, onion and salt. Cover with crushed ice; mix well. Let stand 3 hours. Drain; rinse and drain thoroughly.

2. In a Dutch oven, combine sugar, water, vinegars, mustard seed, celery seed and peppercorns. Bring to a boil, stirring to dissolve sugar. Add cucumber mixture; return to a boil, stirring occasionally. Reduce heat; simmer, uncovered, 4-5 minutes or until heated through.

3. Carefully ladle hot mixture into 4 hot wide-mouth 1-pint jars, leaving ½-in. headspace. Add 3 garlic cloves and 1 bay leaf to each jar. Remove air bubbles and, if necessary, adjust headspace by adding hot pickling liquid. Wipe rims. Center lids on jars; screw on bands until fingertip tight.

4. Place jars into canner with simmering water, ensuring they are completely covered with water. Bring to a boil; process for 10 minutes. Remove jars and cool.

¼ **CUP** 35 cal., 0 fat (0 sat. fat), 0 chol., 175mg sod., 8g carb. (7g sugars, 0 fiber), 0 pro.

Sweet Rewards of Giving Back

A busy mom's syrup business helps
feed hungry children around the world.

BY JILL GLEESON

Nadia Khan loves kids. Even though she has five of her own, ranging in age from 3 to 18, it's clear she keeps space in her heart for all the world's children.

Since founding Wäbry Organic Syrups in 2015, she's donated a portion of the sale of each bottle to help feed orphaned youth. Nadia estimates that her company is responsible for serving some 30,000 meals to children through the GiveLight Foundation, which provides care to orphans in 10 developing countries and the United States.

Nadia, who lives with her family in the Los Angeles area, began making her syrups as a way of encouraging her 2-year-old to drink milk.

"As a child, I used to love strawberry milk," she says, "but it was that kind with high-fructose corn syrup and no real fruit. I didn't feel comfortable giving that to my son. So I bought some organic strawberries, chopped them up and boiled them with organic sugar. It was really good! In fact, when I mixed it into his milk, he loved it so much that he asked for more."

Left: Nadia Khan created a strawberry syrup to encourage her son Hasan to drink more milk. He loves it in a snow cone, too!

Pretty soon Nadia's family and friends were putting her syrup on pancakes and on yogurt. Her husband loved it, too, and added it to sparkling water topped off with a scoop of vanilla ice cream to make a float.

After a lot of encouragement from her devoted fans, Nadia founded Wäbry Organic Syrups, the name inspired by how her son pronounced "strawberry." Today the company offers a variety of flavors, as well as syrups with no added sugar. She sells mostly through Amazon, although the syrups are also available at a few retailers in California, Colorado and New York. Nadia says she is most thankful for her ability to help kids.

"Every time I put my check to GiveLight in the mail, which I do every four months," she says, "I feel an overwhelming sense of gratitude that because of this business we are able to feed more children together than I would have been able to feed alone. For me, giving back isn't just incidental. It's one of the reasons I started this business. And it's something my husband and I and our kids remind each other of when the workload is particularly busy or stressful—our efforts will directly impact the lives of underprivileged kids, and that's an honor." ♦

Fourth of July

Flag Wall Hanging

A humble handkerchief gets a cheery new
look in this project.

WHAT YOU'LL NEED

- **Four 22-in.-sq.
  red bandannas**
- **Three 22-in.-sq.
  white bandannas**
- **One 22-in.-sq.
  blue bandanna**
- **Coordinating thread**

- **26-in. dowel rod**
- **Twine**
- **13 star-shaped lapel pins**
- **Scissors**
- **Sewing machine**
- **Iron**
- **Straight pins**

DIRECTIONS

1. Wash and dry bandannas.
2. Cut red and white bandannas into 5-in.-wide strips. Sew 2 red
   strips together at short ends. Repeat with remaining red pieces
   for 7 long strips. Repeat with white pieces for 6 long strips.
3. Fold 1½ in. of raw edge on each side of each strip to back and
   press in place with iron, leaving 2-in.-wide strip.
4. Fold 3 in. of each strip over the dowel rod and pin in place with
   straight pins, alternating red and white stripes.
5. Fold blue bandanna to match width of 7 stripes (approximately
   14 in.). Fold over dowel, covering left 7 stripes and adjusting
   to desired length. Secure with straight pins.
6. Cut 30 in. of twine and tie around ends of dowel to hang.
7. Insert star-shaped pins at top of each stripe to secure. Remove
   straight pins.

Star Lights

These festive luminaries are
as much fun as fireworks.

WHAT YOU'LL NEED

- **Spray paint, optional**
- **3 quart-sized Mason jars with lids with wire hangers**
- **Star stickers or card stock and adhesive sheet**
- **Red, white and blue acrylic craft paint**
- **Decoupage glue**
- **3 tea lights or 3 strings of battery-operated mini lights**
- **Small paintbrush**

· ·

DIRECTIONS

1. Spray-paint lids, if desired. Dry thoroughly.
2. If needed, draw a template of a star shape on card stock and use to cut out star stickers from adhesive sheet. Cover jars in a decorative pattern with stickers.
3. Paint 1 jar red, 1 white and 1 blue with acrylic paint. Dry thoroughly. Repeat with a second coat of paint.
4. Carefully remove stickers. Touch up paint as needed and dry thoroughly.
5. Paint a coat of decoupage glue over each jar and dry thoroughly.
6. Insert lights into jars. Top with lids.

Firecracker Napkins

Make your place settings pop with these sparkling roll-ups.

WHAT YOU'LL NEED (FOR EACH NAPKIN)

- **Bandanna**
- **18-in. piece of twine**
- **Firework swizzle stick**

DIRECTIONS

1. First, fold a bandanna in half, and then in half 2 more times.
2. Next, fold the bottom edge of the bandanna to the left. Starting with that end, roll it all the way up.
3. Wrap an 18-in. piece of twine around the bandanna and secure it with a knot.
4. Place a firework swizzle stick in the center of the roll.

Root Beer Pulled Pork Nachos

I count on my slow cooker to do the honors when I have a house full of summer guests. Teenagers especially love DIY nachos.

—James Schend, Pleasant Prairie, WI

Prep **20 min.** ◆ Cook **8 hours** ◆ Makes **12 servings**

WHAT YOU'LL NEED

- 1 boneless pork shoulder butt roast (3 to 4 lbs.)
- 1 can (12 oz.) root beer or cola
- 12 cups tortilla chips
- 2 cups shredded cheddar cheese
- 2 medium tomatoes, chopped
  Optional: Pico de gallo, chopped green onions and sliced jalapeno peppers

DIRECTIONS

1. In a 4- or 5-qt. slow cooker, combine pork roast and root beer. Cook, covered, on low 8-9 hours, until meat is tender.

2. Remove roast; cool slightly. When cool enough to handle, shred meat with 2 forks. Return to slow cooker; keep warm.

3. To serve, drain pork. Layer tortilla chips with pork, cheese, tomatoes and optional toppings as desired. Serve immediately.

1 SERVING 391 cal., 23g fat (8g sat. fat), 86mg chol., 287mg sod., 20g carb. (4g sugars, 1g fiber), 25g pro.

 Tip Try cola, ginger ale or lemon-lime soda if you're not into root beer.

Juicy Lucy

Friends in Minnesota introduced me to the Juicy Lucy burger, a local favorite. Instead of putting the cheese on top, it gets stuffed inside, keeping the meat around the cheese nice and juicy.

—Brigette Kutschma, Lake Geneva, WI

Takes **30 min.** ◆ Makes **4 servings**

WHAT YOU'LL NEED

- **1 lb. ground beef**
- **8 Tbsp. shredded American or cheddar cheese**
- **½ tsp. salt**
- **½ tsp. pepper**
- **4 hamburger buns, split and toasted**
- **Optional: Tomato slices, onion slices, lettuce**

DIRECTIONS

1. Shape beef into 8 thin patties. Divide cheese among 4 patties; top with remaining patties and press edges firmly to seal. Sprinkle with salt and pepper.

2. Grill burgers, covered, over medium heat or broil 4 in. from heat until a thermometer reads 160° and juices run clear, 6-8 minutes on each side. Serve on buns with toppings of your choice.

1 BURGER 376 cal., 19g fat (8g sat. fat), 84mg chol., 756mg sod., 23g carb. (4g sugars, 1g fiber), 27g pro.

Stuffed Grilled Zucchini

Pair these zucchini boats with charred pork chops,
smoked fish and other grilled greats.

—Nancy Zimmerman, Cape May Court House, NJ

Prep **25 min.** ◆ Grill **10 min.** ◆ Makes **4 servings**

WHAT YOU'LL NEED

- **4** medium zucchini
- **5** tsp. olive oil, divided
- **2** Tbsp. finely chopped red onion
- **¼** tsp. minced garlic
- **½** cup dry bread crumbs
- **½** cup shredded part-skim mozzarella cheese
- **1** Tbsp. minced fresh mint
- **½** tsp. salt
- **3** Tbsp. grated Parmesan cheese

DIRECTIONS

1. Cut zucchini in half lengthwise; scoop out flesh, leaving ¼-in. shells. Brush with 2 tsp. oil; set aside. Chop zucchini flesh.

2. In a large skillet, saute flesh and onion in remaining oil. Add garlic; cook 1 minute longer. Add bread crumbs; cook and stir until golden brown, about 2 minutes.

3. Remove from heat. Stir in mozzarella cheese, mint and salt. Spoon into zucchini shells. Sprinkle with Parmesan cheese.

4. Grill, covered, over medium heat until zucchini is tender, 8-10 minutes.

2 STUFFED ZUCCHINI HALVES 186 cal., 10g fat (3g sat. fat), 11mg chol., 553mg sod., 17g carb. (4g sugars, 3g fiber), 9g pro. **DIABETIC EXCHANGES** 1 vegetable, 1 lean meat, 1 fat, ½ starch.

Red, White & Blueberry Poke Cake

A sweet treat in the summer, this patriotic poke cake with dazzling red and blue stripes is a fun one to make with the kids.

—Elisabeth Schulz, Blossvale, NY

Prep **40 min.** + cooling ◆ Bake **25 min.** + chilling ◆ Makes **12 servings**

WHAT YOU'LL NEED

- **1** pkg. white cake mix (regular size)
- **1¼** cups water
- **2** large eggs, room temperature
- **¼** cup canola oil

STRAWBERRY GELATIN
- **1** cup fresh strawberries
- **⅔** cup sugar
- **¼** cup water
- **2¼** tsp. strawberry gelatin

BLUEBERRY GELATIN
- **¾** cup fresh blueberries
- **½** cup water
- **4½** tsp. sugar
- **4½** tsp. berry blue gelatin

FROSTING AND FILLING
- **2½** cups heavy whipping cream
- **⅓** cup confectioners' sugar

DIRECTIONS

1. Preheat oven to 350°. Line bottoms of two 9-in. round baking pans with parchment or waxed paper; coat paper with cooking spray. In a large bowl, combine cake mix, water, eggs and oil; beat on low speed 30 seconds. Beat on medium 2 minutes.

2. Transfer to prepared pans. Bake 25-30 minutes or until a toothpick inserted in center comes out clean. Cool completely in pans on wire racks.

3. For strawberry gelatin, in a small saucepan, combine strawberries, sugar and water; bring to a boil. Reduce heat; simmer, uncovered, 2-3 minutes or until berries are soft. Strain into a small bowl, pressing berries lightly; discard pulp. Add gelatin to syrup, stirring to dissolve completely. Cool to room temperature. Repeat steps to make blueberry gelatin.

4. Using a wooden skewer, pierce tops of cakes to within 1 in. of edge; twist skewer gently to make slightly larger holes. Gradually pour cooled strawberry mixture over 1 cake, being careful to fill each hole. Repeat with blueberry mixture and remaining cake. Refrigerate, covered, overnight.

5. In a large bowl, beat cream until it begins to

thicken. Add confectioners' sugar; beat until soft peaks form.

6. Run a knife around sides of pans to loosen cakes. Remove strawberry cake from pan; remove paper. Place cake on a serving plate. Spread with 1 cup whipped cream.

7. Remove blueberry cake from pan; remove paper. Place cake over whipped cream layer. Frost top and sides with remaining cream. Refrigerate at least 1 hour before serving.

1 PIECE 477 cal., 28g fat (13g sat. fat), 100mg chol., 328mg sod., 55g carb. (38g sugars, 0 fiber), 4g pro.

NOTE A poke cake is so-called because you poke holes in it before pouring a liquid topping over it.

Brownie Waffle
Ice Cream Sundaes

My four young girls bake brownies completely on their own.
This summer, we experimented with our brownie batter
in the waffle iron and served it with ice cream!

—Juliana Evans, Wesley Chapel, FL

Prep **15 min.** ◆ Bake **5 min./batch** ◆ Makes **8 servings**

WHAT YOU'LL NEED

- ½ **cup unsalted butter**
- 1 **cup sugar**
- ⅓ **cup baking cocoa**
- 1 **tsp. vanilla extract**
- 2 **large eggs,
  room temperature**
- ½ **cup all-purpose flour**
- ½ **tsp. salt**
- 4 **cups vanilla ice cream
  Optional: Chocolate
  ice cream topping
  and sprinkles**

DIRECTIONS

1. Preheat a round Belgian waffle maker. In a microwave, melt butter on high, stirring every 30 seconds. Stir in sugar, cocoa and vanilla. Add eggs, 1 at a time, whisking after each addition. Add flour and salt; stir just until combined.

2. Bake waffles according to manufacturer's directions until cooked through, 4-5 minutes. Let stand on open waffle maker for 30-60 seconds to crisp up before carefully removing.

3. Cut waffles into fourths. Top each wedge with a scoop of ice cream. If desired, add ice cream topping and sprinkles.

¼ **WAFFLE WITH ½ CUP ICE CREAM** 394 cal., 20g fat (12g sat. fat), 106mg chol., 220mg sod., 49g carb. (39g sugars, 1g fiber), 5g pro.

Red, White & Blue Frozen Lemonade

This patriotic drink is as pretty as it is delicious. With cherries, blueberries and lemon juice, we created a striped lemonade that is perfect for a Fourth of July celebration.

—Shawn Carleton, San Diego, CA

Takes **10 min.** ◆ Makes **4 servings**

WHAT YOU'LL NEED

1 cup lemon juice
1 cup sugar
4 cups ice cubes
1 cup fresh or frozen blueberries
Maraschino cherries

DIRECTIONS

1. Place lemon juice, sugar and ice in a blender; cover and process until slushy.
2. Divide blueberries among 4 chilled glasses; muddle slightly.
3. Add lemon slush; top with cherries.

¾ **CUP** 229 cal., 0 fat (0 sat. fat), 0 chol., 1mg sod., 60g carb. (55g sugars, 1g fiber), 0 pro.

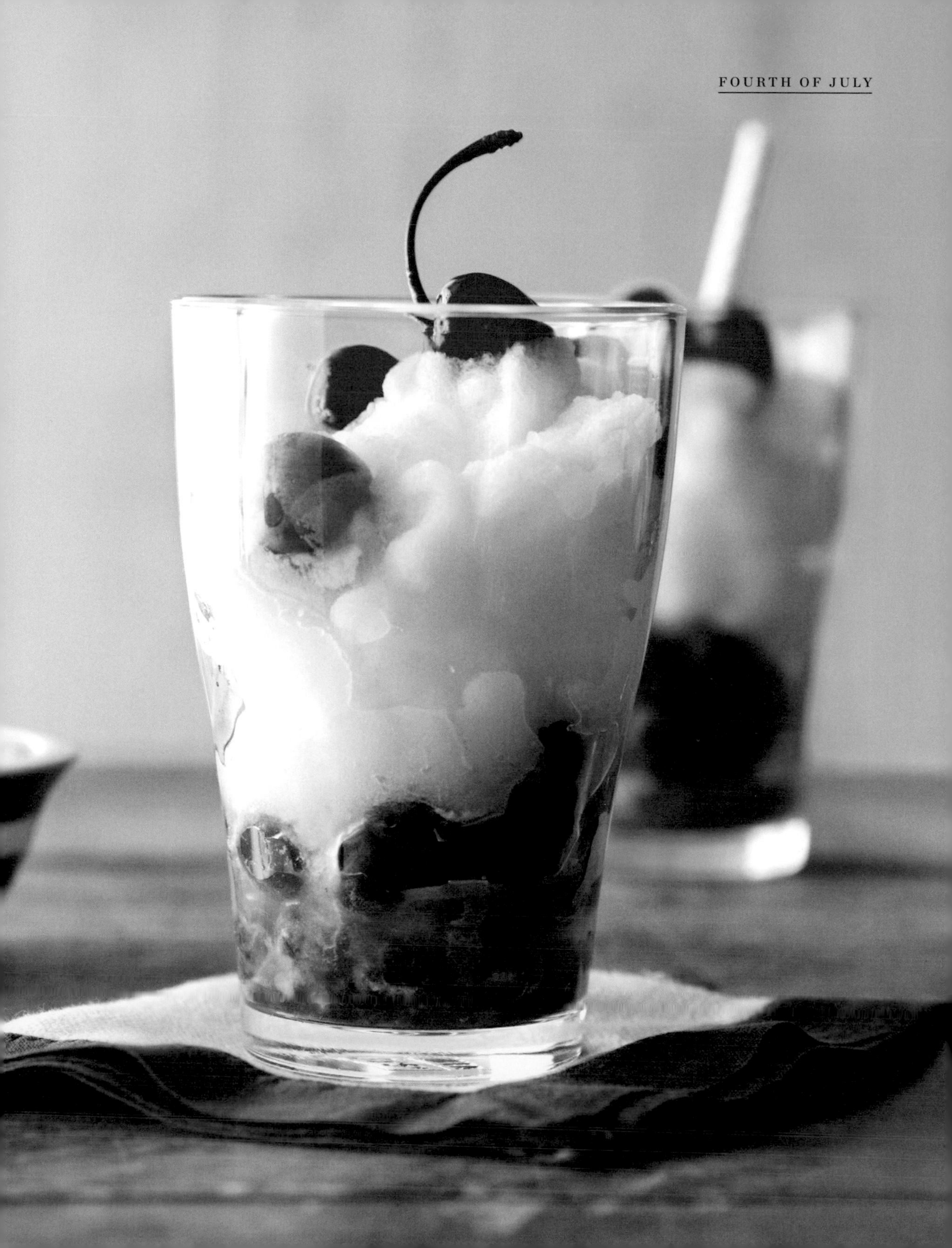

Star-Spangled Farms

America celebrates its independence on the Fourth of July. See how growers across the country raise Old Glory year-round.

1. PASTORAL PATRIOTISM

My beloved granddaughter Kristen Wineinger took this photo of a patriotic barn just a few miles from my home. There are always lots of American flags flying in this neighborhood, and even more around July Fourth.
Meta Stavrand, Highland Lakes, NJ

2. FAMILY TRADITIONS

My cousin Hannah rides her horse at our family's Fourth of July celebration. Each year we gather at the farm to honor those who made the ultimate sacrifice for our freedom.
Jonna Stevens, Conway, SC

3. A LUCKY FIND
Driving in the countryside near my Wisconsin hometown, I took a wrong turn; as I turned back to the road, I spotted this pallet in a farmyard and grabbed my camera.
Bill Chizek, El Paso, TX

4. RED, WHITE AND MOO
The cows check out our red, white and blue here at Rocking G Livestock, a three-generation operation in western North Carolina.
Harriet Gilleland, Taylorsville, NC

5. LET FREEDOM RING
What's not to love? A garden in bloom, a sunny day and a big red barn dressed up for the holiday. Happy Fourth of July!
Terry Wild, Lexington, KY

6. FOND OF THE FARM

I've photographed this barn at Sweetwater Farm on Martha's Vineyard many times over the years; it's one of my favorites. Of course, it's even better when the horses are out.

Paul Rezendes, Royalston, MA

7. PAYING RESPECTS

Every year our family volunteers to place flags on veterans' graves. I took this photo as ROTC cadets passed our youngest daughter, Madison.

Gerry Eisert, Papillion, NE

8. FROM SEA TO SHINING SEA

My husband, Lyle, and his brother, Gordon, painted the flag on our barn. Lyle and I have visited all 50 states; we take the back roads so we can get a look at every corner of America.

Shirley Stuby, Schellsburg, PA

Special of the Day

Belly laughs were the secret ingredient in this
memorable meal.

BY VERNA SIMMS

One Fourth of July, before the United States entered World War II, I decided to make a special supper for my husband, Howard, and myself before we went out. We planned to spend the evening watching fireworks and eating homemade ice cream. I looked around the kitchen for something to prepare, and I found a modest steak in the freezer.

"Funny, I don't recall freezing a steak," I thought.

I heard the screen door open, and a faint whiff of Howard's mare wafted in. My husband spent hours grooming his horse, and I could often smell the result before I saw it.

"What are you planning, honeybunch?" Howard said.

"I found a small steak in the freezer," I said. "It shouldn't take long to prepare. I could go out back and pick a mess of string beans, maybe scratch around the roots of the potato vines to find a new potato or two while the steak is defrosting. With a bit of milk gravy and sourdough biscuits, that should do. Think you might pick a ripe tomato or two?"

I headed outside to gather the string beans and potatoes. Returning to the house carrying the produce in my apron, I nearly dropped everything when I heard my husband's raucous laughter coming from the kitchen. I rushed in to see what was happening.

"What's funny?" I asked him. "Share the joke."

"The steak," Howard sputtered, laughing. "I was preparing to sprinkle it with tenderizer. " He held it under my nose.

"Oh my gosh—that's not even meat," I said with disappointment. "It's that old washcloth I froze to use as an ice pack."

"Look at the funny side," he said. "Slip on your new dress and we'll mosey down the road to Mom and Pop's Restaurant. I've heard they serve fantastic steak. We don't even need to tap into your egg money; I can handle it."

Later, sitting under a tree before the fireworks started, I reached for Howard's hand.

"Well, you were right on both counts," I said. "Mom and Pop's does make a scrumptious steak. And the washcloth was hilarious."

As the sky burst into many colored lights, we both erupted in laughter. ♦

Summer Gatherings

A Better Backyard Bash

Celebrate your independence from the same-old barbecues with the best tips on the block.

1. PULL-ALONG PARTY

Cool drinks are a must at a summer party. Place bottled sippers into a clean red wagon filled with ice for a cuter take on a cooler. "Kids love pulling it around," says blogger Loralee Lewis of loraleelewis.com. "It's free beverage service!"

2. TOPPER TIN

Use a muffin tin to double as a handy condiment caddy. Fill each compartment with your favorite toppings and add mini serving spoons so guests can load up their burgers and dogs as they like.

3. BAN THE BUZZ

Shoo bugs from the scene with a pretty pot of herbs. "Plants like lavender, mint, rue and tansy have been used to repel insects for ages," says Briscoe White, co-owner of The Growers Exchange, thegrowers-exchange.com.

Dress Up Drab

The ideas on these pole barns and farm sheds
will conceal boring, bare walls in no time.

1. BIRD TREE

For a whimsical scene that'll take a backyard
shed well past the growing season, consider
garden art. Here, designers at Bachman's
garden center in Minneapolis, Minnesota,
attached reclaimed wood and ceramic and
wooden birdhouses to the wall with screws.

2. PETAL POWER

On the other side of the same shed, brightly
colored hoses and painted tube pans were
tacked to the wall with metal brackets to
create oversize flowers.

3. PLANTS ADD PUNCH

Brenda Barr of Blanchester, Ohio, placed two
sections of picket fencing against her barn,
behind a stand of black-eyed Susan. "I've had
this old wagon wheel for 30 years," she says.

Potted Crudite

Fill a pot to the brim with bean dip and plant a bunch
of veggies in it for your next party. Then dig in.

—Country Woman *Staff*

Takes **10 min.** ◆ Makes **1 serving**

WHAT YOU'LL NEED

1 **Plastic food storage container to fit inside plant pot (see Note)**
1 **Small clean plant pot**
  Prepared black bean dip
  Assorted fresh vegetables such as baby carrots, broccoli florets, cauliflower florets, cherry tomatoes, radishes, Brussels sprouts
  Fresh herbs, optional
  Chopped ripe olives
1 **Small plate or saucer**

DIRECTIONS

1. Place the plastic food storage container inside plant pot. Fill plastic container with dip, using a spatula to smooth out the top of the dip.

2. Arrange vegetables on top of dip to create a garden patch. Gently open leaves of Brussels sprouts to resemble cabbage. If desired, poke a hole in the top of each carrot and tomato, then insert a sprig of fresh parsley, dill, marjoram, cilantro or oregano.

3. Sprinkle chopped olives around arranged vegetables. Place plant pot on a saucer and serve.

NOTE If your plastic food storage container sits too low in the plant pot, put some small stones in the bottom of the pot and set the container on top of them.

¼ **CUP BLACK BEAN DIP** 70 cal., 2g fat (0 sat. fat), 0 chol., 200mg sod., 10g carb. (0 sugars, 2g fiber), 2g pro.

 Tip Serve extra nibbles, such as crunchy breadsticks, on the side for dipping.

Slow-Cooker Sloppy Joes

On hot summer days, this dish cooks without heating up the kitchen. The recipe is easy to double or triple for crowds.

—Carol Losier, Baldwinsville, NY

Prep **20 min.** ◆ Cook **3 hours** ◆ Makes **8 servings**

WHAT YOU'LL NEED

- 1½ **lbs. ground beef**
- 2 **celery ribs, chopped**
- 1 **small onion, chopped**
- 1 **bottle (12 oz.) chili sauce**
- 2 **Tbsp. brown sugar**
- 2 **Tbsp. sweet pickle relish**
- 1 **Tbsp. Worcestershire sauce**
- 1 **tsp. salt**
- ⅛ **tsp. pepper**
- 8 **hamburger buns, split**

DIRECTIONS

1. In a large skillet, cook beef, celery and onion over medium-high heat, 8-10 minutes, until beef is no longer pink, breaking beef into crumbles; drain. Transfer to a 3-qt. slow cooker.

2. Stir in chili sauce, brown sugar, pickle relish, Worcestershire sauce, salt and pepper. Cook, covered, on low 3-4 hours or until heated through and flavors are blended. Spoon meat mixture onto bun bottoms. Replace tops.

1 SANDWICH 324 cal., 10g fat (4g sat. fat), 42mg chol., 1313mg sod., 40g carb. (16g sugars, 1g fiber), 19g pro.

Spaghetti Squash & Sausage Easy Meal

My son's favorite dish uses homegrown spaghetti squash, kielbasa, and pico de gallo or salsa.

—Pam Mascarenas, Taylorsville, UT

....

Takes **30 min.** ◆ Makes **6 servings**

....

WHAT YOU'LL NEED

- 1 medium spaghetti squash
- 1 Tbsp. olive oil
- 1 pkg. (14 oz.) smoked sausage, halved lengthwise and sliced
- 1 cup pico de gallo
- ¼ tsp. salt
- ⅛ tsp. pepper

DIRECTIONS

1. Cut squash lengthwise in half; discard seeds. Place halves on a microwave-safe plate, cut side down. Microwave, uncovered, on high 15-20 minutes or until tender.
2. Meanwhile, in a large skillet, heat oil over medium heat. Add sausage; cook and stir 4-5 minutes or until lightly browned.
3. When squash is cool enough to handle, use a fork to separate strands. Add squash, pico de gallo, salt and pepper to sausage; heat through, tossing to combine.

1 CUP 326 cal., 22g fat (8g sat. fat), 44mg chol., 901mg sod., 24g carb. (2g sugars, 5g fiber), 12g pro.

Asparagus Bruschetta

I really like asparagus, so I'm always trying it in different things.
This is a delicious twist on traditional bruschetta.

—Elaine Sweet, Dallas, TX

Takes **30 min.** ◆ Makes **1 dozen**

WHAT YOU'LL NEED

- ½ lb. fresh asparagus, trimmed and cut into ½-in. pieces
- 2 cups grape tomatoes, halved
- ¼ cup minced fresh basil
- 3 green onions, chopped
- 3 Tbsp. lime juice
- 1 Tbsp. olive oil
- 3 garlic cloves, minced
- 1½ tsp. grated lime zest
- ¼ tsp. salt
- ¼ tsp. pepper
- 12 slices French bread baguette (½ in. thick), toasted
- ½ cup crumbled blue cheese

DIRECTIONS

1. In a large saucepan, bring 3 cups water to a boil. Add the asparagus; cover and boil for 2-4 minutes. Drain and immediately place asparagus in ice water. Drain and pat dry.
2. In a large bowl, combine asparagus, tomatoes, basil, onions, lime juice, oil, garlic, lime zest, salt and pepper. Using a slotted spoon, spoon asparagus mixture onto toasted bread slices. Sprinkle with blue cheese.

1 PIECE 88 cal., 3g fat (1g sat. fat), 4mg chol., 237mg sod., 13g carb. (1g sugars, 1g fiber), 3g pro. **DIABETIC EXCHANGES** 1 starch, ½ fat.

New England Baked Beans

For a potluck or picnic, you can't beat this classic side. Molasses and maple syrup give it a slight sweetness.

—Pat Medeiros, Tiverton, RI

Prep **1½ hours + soaking** ◆ Bake **2½ hours** ◆ Makes **12 servings**

WHAT YOU'LL NEED

- **1 lb. dried great northern beans**
- **½ lb. thick-sliced bacon strips, chopped**
- **2 large onions, chopped**
- **3 garlic cloves, minced**
- **2 cups ketchup**
- **1½ cups packed dark brown sugar**
- **⅓ cup molasses**
- **⅓ cup maple syrup**
- **¼ cup Worcestershire sauce**
- **½ tsp. salt**
- **¼ tsp. coarsely ground pepper**

DIRECTIONS

1. Sort beans and rinse with cold water. Place beans in a Dutch oven; add enough water to cover by 2 in. Bring to a boil; boil for 2 minutes. Remove from the heat; cover and let stand for 1 hour or until beans are softened.

2. Drain and rinse beans, discarding liquid. Return beans to Dutch oven; add 6 cups water. Bring to a boil. Reduce heat; cover and simmer for 1 hour or until beans are almost tender.

3. In a large skillet, cook bacon over medium heat until crisp. Remove to paper towels with a slotted spoon; drain, reserving 2 Tbsp. drippings. Saute onions in drippings until tender. Add garlic; cook 1 minute longer. Stir in the ketchup, brown sugar, molasses, syrup, Worcestershire sauce, salt and pepper.

4. Drain beans, reserving cooking liquid; place in an ungreased 3-qt. baking dish. Stir in onion mixture and bacon. Cover and bake at 300° for 2½ hours or until beans are tender and reach desired consistency, stirring every 30 minutes. Add reserved cooking liquid as needed.

⅔ **CUP** 385 cal., 5g fat (2g sat. fat), 7mg chol., 810mg sod., 77g carb. (50g sugars, 8g fiber), 11g pro.

Strawberry Pretzel Dessert Minis

This make-ahead layered salad, adorable in individual Mason jars, will disappear quickly at any potluck.

—Aldene Belch, Flint, MI

Prep **30 min.** ◆ Bake **15 min. + chilling** ◆ Makes **32 servings**

WHAT YOU'LL NEED

- **2** cups crushed pretzels (about 8 oz.)
- **¾** cup butter, melted
- **3** Tbsp. sugar

FILLING
- **2** cups whipped topping
- **1** pkg. (8 oz.) cream cheese, softened
- **1** cup sugar

TOPPING
- **2** pkg. (3 oz. each) strawberry gelatin
- **2** cups boiling water
- **2** pkg. (16 oz. each) frozen sweetened sliced strawberries, thawed

DIRECTIONS

1. Preheat oven to 350°. In a small bowl, combine pretzels, butter and sugar; spread onto a baking sheet. Bake until crisp and lightly browned, 12-15 minutes. Cool completely on a wire rack; break into small pieces.

2. For filling, in a small bowl, beat whipped topping, cream cheese and sugar until smooth. Refrigerate until chilled.

3. For topping, in a large bowl, dissolve gelatin in boiling water. Stir in sweetened strawberries; chill until partially set, about 1 hour. Carefully layer pretzel mixture, filling and topping into 4-oz. glass jars. Chill until firm, at least 2 hours. If desired, serve with additional whipped topping and pretzels.

1 JAR 172 cal., 8g fat (5g sat. fat), 19mg chol., 151mg sod., 25g carb. (20g sugars, 1g fiber), 2g pro.

Zucchini Cupcakes

I asked my grandmother for this recipe after trying these irresistible spice cupcakes at her home.

—Virginia Lapierre, Greensboro Bend, VT

Prep **20 min.** ◆ Bake **20 min. + cooling** ◆ Makes **about 1½ dozen**

WHAT YOU'LL NEED

- 3 large eggs, room temperature
- 1⅓ cups sugar
- ½ cup canola oil
- ½ cup orange juice
- 1 tsp. almond extract
- 2½ cups all-purpose flour
- 2 tsp. ground cinnamon
- 2 tsp. baking powder
- 1 tsp. baking soda
- 1 tsp. salt
- ½ tsp. ground cloves
- 1½ cups shredded zucchini

FROSTING

- 1 cup packed brown sugar
- ½ cup butter, cubed
- ¼ cup 2% milk
- 1 tsp. vanilla extract
- 1½ to 2 cups confectioners' sugar

DIRECTIONS

1. Preheat oven to 350°. Beat together the first 5 ingredients. Combine dry ingredients; gradually add to egg mixture and blend well. Stir in zucchini.

2. Fill paper-lined muffin cups two-thirds full. Bake until a toothpick inserted in center comes out clean, 20-25 minutes. Cool 10 minutes before removing to a wire rack.

3. For frosting, combine brown sugar, butter and milk in a large saucepan. Bring to a boil over medium heat; cook and stir until thickened, 1-2 minutes. Remove from heat; stir in vanilla. Cool to lukewarm.

4. Gradually beat in confectioners' sugar until frosting reaches spreading consistency. Frost the cupcakes.

1 CUPCAKE 327 cal., 12g fat (4g sat. fat), 45mg chol., 305mg sod., 52g carb. (38g sugars, 1g fiber), 3g pro.

Sweet & Salty Party Mix

These crunchy munchies are sure to rank high
with your family and friends.

—Candice Lumley, Charles City, IA

Prep **10 min.** ◆ Bake **1¼ hours + cooling** ◆ Makes **about 10 qt.**

WHAT YOU'LL NEED

- 1 pkg. (12 oz.) Corn Chex
- 1 pkg. (10 oz.) Cheerios
- 1 pkg. (10 oz.) Honeycomb cereal
- 1 pkg. (10 oz.) pretzel sticks
- 1¾ cups sugar
- 1½ cups canola oil
- 1¼ cups butter, melted
- 3 Tbsp. soy sauce
- 2 Tbsp. garlic salt

DIRECTIONS

1. Preheat oven to 275°. In a very large bowl, combine cereals and pretzels. In another bowl, mix the remaining ingredients until sugar is dissolved. Pour over cereal mixture; toss to coat.

2. Transfer to a large roasting pan. Bake, uncovered, 1¼ hours or until the cereal is crisp, stirring every 15 minutes. Cool completely. Store in an airtight container.

¾ CUP 227 cal., 13g fat (4g sat. fat), 13mg chol., 560mg sod., 28g carb. (11g sugars, 1g fiber), 2g pro.

5-Ingredient Fudge

You're moments away from a pan of creamy fudge.
Just microwave, stir and spread.

—Sue Tucker, Edgemoor, SC

Prep **10 min. + chilling** ◆ Makes **about 2⅓ lbs. (81 pieces)**

WHAT YOU'LL NEED

- 1½ tsp. plus 1 Tbsp. butter, divided
- 2 cups semisweet chocolate chips
- 1 pkg. (11½ oz.) milk chocolate chips
- 1 can (14 oz.) sweetened condensed milk
- 1 tsp. vanilla extract

DIRECTIONS

1. Line a 9-in. square pan with foil; grease foil with 1½ tsp. butter.
2. In a large microwave-safe bowl, melt chocolate chips and remaining butter, stirring after 1 minute and every 30 seconds thereafter. Stir in milk and vanilla. Spread into prepared pan. Refrigerate until firm.
3. Using foil, lift fudge out of pan. Remove foil; cut fudge into 1-in. squares. Store in an airtight container in the refrigerator.

1 PIECE 59 cal., 3g fat (2g sat. fat), 3mg chol., 12mg sod., 8g carb. (7g sugars, 0 fiber), 1g pro.

When a Salad Is Not a Salad

Merging two families into one can be flat-out funny.

BY SARAH WHITE

My husband, Hans, grew up in a family that knew the names of lots of weird veggies, as well as how to cook them. When his family members say they're having salad for dinner, they mean salad IS dinner—it will be healthy, with sprouts, nuts and vinegar dressing.

We are more of a meat and potatoes crew in my family. We have veggies with every meal, but they are side dishes.

Without this knowledge, I led my future husband to that minefield known as the meet-the-family dinner. My young son; my parents and sister; my aunt, uncle and cousins; my 90-year-old grandmother; and my fiance and I gathered around a table to indulge in prime rib and sides of baked potatoes, green bean casserole, dinner rolls and our traditional gelatin salad.

There are many ways to make a gelatin salad, but my grandma's version combines applesauce, lemon Jell-O and melted-down cinnamon Red Hots. A middle layer of cream cheese, mayonnaise, walnuts and celery is sandwiched between the Jell-O. When this amazing concoction was presented to Hans, we got a family story we will laugh about for years to come.

"Some salad?" my mother asked him, holding out a Pyrex dish full of delicious, spicy, jiggly redness.

"Yes, please," he replied. He took the dish and looked down.

Uncertainty flashed across his face. His future mother-in-law definitely said "salad." But there was no lettuce to be seen. He wrinkled his brow and lifted the glass dish to check the bottom. No vegetation on the bottom, either.

He cautiously took a spoonful, plopped it on his plate and tried a bite. Everyone at the table paused to watch him chew.

"It's good," he said. "But this is not a salad."

To this day, Hans tells everyone that he married into a family that calls a dessert a salad. No matter what you call it, it's scrumptious. ♦

The Pie and the Preacher

A shortage of dessert got the best of Grandma.

BY DOREEN ROSEVOLD

Early one summer Sunday morning in 1939, my grandmother prepared the family dinner she'd serve after church, as usual. But on the way to the service, she remembered it was her turn to bring the preacher home for dinner. A meal with the preacher was an event in those days, and it usually meant preparing a special menu. Grandma had been so focused on canning her garden produce that she had forgotten about her dinner guest until we were all rolling along the country road in our car on the way to church.

Grandma's mind raced to assess whether she had prepared enough Sunday dinner to include the minister. She decided that she had, but she hadn't made dessert. She worried that if word got out, it would ruin her reputation as a competent wife, mother and member of the congregation. As her thoughts tumbled forward, she recalled the one piece of leftover pie in the refrigerator. But one piece wouldn't be enough to serve eight!

It could serve one, though, Grandma reasoned as she hatched a plan. She told each family member that when she asked if anyone wanted dessert, they were to answer, "No, thank you! I'm just too full!" That way the pastor could have pie—and Grandma's reputation as a capable host could be preserved.

The church service seemed to drag on, and Grandma had trouble concentrating on anything but the dinner she would serve later. Afterward, the minister got into the front seat of the car with the older kids and my grandparents squeezed into the back with the younger ones. When she could safely do so, Grandma whispered a last reminder: "Remember. Don't ask for dessert!"

The dinner went off without a hitch and then the moment arrived—it was time for dessert. My grandmother casually said, "I have apple pie. Who would like a piece for dessert?" A chorus of "No, thank you. I'm too full," echoed in reply, as Grandma had instructed. To her surprise, even the preacher said, "No, thanks. I'm too full, too!"

My grandfather, hearing this unexpected opportunity, said, "I guess I will have a piece of your apple pie, Mother. You make the best pie in the county." He added the last with a dose of admiration that he thought Grandma would appreciate.

Grandma placed the pie in front of Grandpa, who dove in with zeal. "My! That does look delicious," the preacher said. "I guess I'll have some, too!"

My grandma had to confess. And Grandpa didn't get apple pie again for a very long time. ◆

Birthdays

Crafts and Decor

Recipes

Stories

Arrow
Place Cards

A fun way to assign seats, these can also double as
party favors that are sure to hit the target!

WHAT YOU'LL NEED

- Acrylic paint
- 7-in. twig pencils, set of
  12 (available online and
  at World Market) (see note)
- Scrap paper
- 3 sheets of 12x9-in. felt
- 5-in. feathers
- (about 5 per pencil)
- Card stock
- Twine
- Paintbrush
- Glue gun
- Craft punch in heart or
  tag shape

DIRECTIONS

1. Paint stripes on twig pencils; let dry.
2. Cut two 3-in. triangles from scrap paper. Hot glue 2 sides
   together and check to make sure the arrowhead fits over the
   sharpened end of a pencil. Adjust size, if necessary, then use
   paper arrowhead as a template to cut 2 felt triangles per pencil.
   Hot glue arrowhead pieces together at long angled sides,
   leaving short side open. Slip felt arrowheads over sharpened
   ends of pencils.
3. Hot glue feathers at the top ends of each pencil.
4. Punch tags from card stock and attach to pencils with twine.

   NOTE Pencils come presharpened. Use with caution around very
   young children.

Gift-Wrap Organizer

Dress up all your presents
with the tools in this handy caddy.

WHAT YOU'LL NEED

- **60-in.-wide upholstery fabric:**
  1 yd. of solid for background and
  ½ yd. of print for pockets and trim
- **1 yd. of 54-in.-wide 4-gauge**
  clear vinyl
- **All-purpose matching thread**
- **Two 10½x13½-in. pieces of**
  clear plastic canvas
- **Coordinating fabric ribbon:**
  3½ yds. of ⅞-in.-wide ribbon
  for trim on pockets and 1½ yds.
  of ¼-in.-wide ribbon for spool
  and scissors holders
- **12½-in. length of ⅝-in.-wide**
  hook-and-loop tape
- **27-in.-long curtain rod for hanger**
- **21-40-in. adjustable sash rod**
  for ribbon holder
- **Standard sewing supplies**

DIRECTIONS

1. From solid upholstery fabric, cut two 29x30-in. pieces for front and back of organizer. Overcast all edges of each piece. Fold 1 in. along 30-in. sides of each piece to wrong side. Topstitch close to raw edges and ¼ in. from fold for hem. Set a piece aside for back.

2. From print upholstery fabric, cut two 14x12-in. pieces for gift-wrap pocket and two 9¾x12-in. pieces for tissue pocket. Also cut a 2½x25½-in. piece for trim on bow container and a 2½x13½-in. piece for trim on tape container.

3. From vinyl, cut one 8x12-in. piece for pocket on front of gift-wrap pocket, one 6x7-in. piece for pocket on front of tissue pocket, two 7½x13-in. pieces for bow container and two 5x7-in. pieces for tape container. Also cut one 20x24-in. piece for gift-wrap rolls.

GIFT-WRAP POCKET

4. Center 8x12-in. vinyl pocket piece on right side of one 14x12-in. gift-wrap pocket piece. Sew ¼ in. from the 2 short edges and 1 long edge. Sew down center to make 2 pockets on the front. Place the 2 gift-wrap pocket pieces together with right sides facing and edges matching. Sew top and side edges together with a ¼-in. seam. Turn right

side out. Insert 13½x10½-in. plastic canvas piece inside pocket.

5. Slide plastic canvas up to top of pocket and sew along pocket bottom to close pocket. Trim, leaving a ¼-in. seam allowance. Overcast the raw edges together.

6. Referring to layout diagram (see page 215) for position, place gift-wrap pocket on organizer front piece, with vinyl pocket facing right side out. Sew bottom edge of gift-wrap pocket to front of organizer with a ¼-in. seam.

RIBBON TRIM

7. Flip pocket up. Mark top edge and sides of pocket. Flip pocket down again.

8. Center and sew a 2-yd. length of ⅞-in.-wide ribbon 3 in. from top-edge line. Flip pocket up and tie ends of ribbon to secure pocket. Trim ribbon ends as desired.

TISSUE POCKET

9. Center 6x7-in. piece of vinyl pocket piece on right side of 1 tissue pocket piece. Sew ¼ in. from 2 long edges and 1 short edge. Place the 2 tissue pocket pieces together with right sides facing and edges matching. Sew top and side edges together with a ¼-in. seam. Turn right side out.

10. Cut piece of plastic canvas to fit, and insert plastic canvas piece inside pocket. Slide plastic canvas piece

up to top of pocket piece and sew along bottom, near plastic canvas piece, to close pocket. Trim, leaving a ¼-in. seam allowance. Overcast raw edges together.

11. Referring to the layout diagram (see page 215 for position), place tissue pocket on organizer front piece, with vinyl pocket facing right side out. Sew bottom edge of tissue pocket to front of organizer with a ¼-in. seam.

RIBBON TRIM

12. Following instructions for gift-wrap pocket trim, sew a 1½-yd. length of ⅞-in.-wide ribbon to front of organizer.

BOW CONTAINER

13. Place the two 7½x13-in. pieces of vinyl together with edges matching.

14. Sew the 7½-in. edges together with a ¼-in. seam for the sides.

15. Sew the 13-in. edges together with a ¼-in. seam for the bottom.

16. Finger-press seams in opposite direction. Align side seams with bottom seam (as shown in Fig. 1 on page 215). Sew 1½ in. from point of triangle on each side. Trim, leaving a ¼-in. seam allowance.

17. Turn right side out.

TRIM

18. Sew short ends of 2½x25½-in. piece of trim together with a ¼-in. seam.

Press seam open. Fold the trim piece in half lengthwise to make a 1½-in.-wide piece.

19. Cut an 8½-in. length of hook-and-loop tape. Sew hook side of tape centered over seam on trim.

20. Slip trim piece over top edge of bow container with hook side of tape facing the outside of the bow container and raw edges matching. Sew in place with a ¼-in. seam. Flip trim piece up so tape is on the outside.

21. Referring to layout diagram (see page 215) for position, sew matching piece of hook-and-loop tape to front of organizer.

TAPE CONTAINER

22. Place two 5x7-in. pieces of vinyl together with edges matching.

23. Sew the 5-in. edges together with a ¼-in. seam for the sides.

24. Sew the 7-in. edges together with a ¼-in. seam for the bottom.

25. Finger-press seams in opposite direction. Flatten corners to make triangular points. Align the bottom seam and side seam as shown in Fig. 1 (see page 215). Sew 1 in. from point of triangle on each side. Trim seam to ¼ in.

26. Turn right side out

TRIM

27. Sew short ends of 2½x13½-in. piece

of trim together with a ¼-in. seam. Press seam open and fold trim piece in half lengthwise to make a 1¼-in.-wide piece.

28. Cut a 4-in. length of hook-and-loop tape. Sew hook side of tape centered over seam of trim.

29. Slip trim piece over top edge of tape container with hook side of tape facing the outside of the tape container and raw edges matching. Sew in place with a ¼-in. seam. Flip trim piece up so tape is on the outside.

30. Referring to layout diagram (see page 215) for position, sew matching piece of hook-and-loop tape to front of organizer.

SCISSORS HOLDER

31. Cut 12-in. length of ¼-in.-wide ribbon.

32. Referring to layout diagram (see page 215) for position, sew center of ribbon to front of organizer.

SPOOL HOLDER

33. Cut two 18-in. lengths of the ¼-in.-wide grosgrain.

34. Referring to layout diagram (see page 215), sew center of each ribbon piece to front of organizer.

GIFT WRAP ROLL POCKET

35. Fold 20x24-in. piece of vinyl in half crosswise to make a 12x20-in. rectangle.

36. Sew raw edges opposite fold together with a ¼-in. seam.
37. With raw edges matching, center vinyl rectangle along bottom edge of front of organizer. Sew to organizer with a ½-in. seam.

ASSEMBLY

38. Pin front and back pieces of organizer together, right sides facing and edges matching. Gift-wrap roll vinyl pocket will be sandwiched between front and back pieces.
39. Sew along bottom and top edges with a ½-in. seam. Turn right side out. Press along seam lines, making sure side edges are aligned. Topstitch through all layers ¼ in. from seam and again 1 in. from bottom seam. Topstitch through all layers ¼ in. from top seam and again to form a channel for the curtain rod.
40. Sew through front and back pieces from side to side about 3½ and 13½ in. from bottom edge to make an interior pocket for gift bags. Be careful not to sew through the gift-wrap and tissue pockets.
41. Press hook-and-loop tape on bow and tape containers to hold to organizer's front.
42. Place scissors over ribbon and knot to hold. Tie ribbon ends in a small bow. Trim ribbon ends as desired.
43. Slip spools of ribbon onto adjustable sash rod. Thread 1 end of each ribbon piece through the hole on each end of the sash rod. Tie ends together in a small bow to hold. Trim ribbon ends as desired.
44. Insert curtain rod in top channel.
45. Place flat-fold paper, tissue paper, gift tags and cards into pockets on front. Slip gift bag into openings between front and back layers.

Tips

TIPS FOR SEWING CLEAR VINYL

- To increase visibility, cut a paper pattern for each piece and slip it under the vinyl.
- Use a rotary cutter and quilter's ruler when cutting.
- Use a roller presser foot or a Teflon foot on your machine. Don't have either? Place gift-wrap transparent tape on the bottom of your presser foot and cut an opening in it for thread. Or cut strips of tissue and place them over seam lines as you sew to reduce drag. Remove paper after stitching.
- Use a long stitch (3.0) and tie threads off rather than backstitching.
- Creases and wrinkles can be removed by warming the vinyl with a blow dryer.

Chocolate Soda

This old-fashioned ice cream soda
pairs perfectly with birthday cake.

—Taste of Home *Test Kitchen*

Takes **5 min.** ◆ Makes **1 serving**

WHAT YOU'LL NEED

- **3 Tbsp. chocolate syrup**
- **1 Tbsp. half-and-half cream**
- **¾ cup carbonated water**
- **¼ cup vanilla ice cream**

DIRECTIONS

1. In a tall glass, combine the chocolate syrup and cream.
2. Stir in water; top with ice cream. Serve immediately.

1¼ CUPS 236 cal., 5g fat (3g sat. fat), 22mg chol., 71mg sod., 44g carb. (36g sugars, 0 fiber), 3g pro.

Cheesecake Pops

The possibilities are endless with these cute cheesecake bites. Customize them for any occasion by using different toppings.

—Evelyn Moore, Elk Grove, CA

Prep **2 hours + freezing** ◆ Makes **45 cheesecake pops**

WHAT YOU'LL NEED

- 3 pkg. (8 oz. each) cream cheese, softened
- 1 cup sugar
- 1 cup sour cream
- 1 tsp. vanilla extract
- 3 large eggs, lightly beaten
- 1 cup graham cracker crumbs
- 45 lollipop sticks (4 in. long)
- 3 pkg. (10 to 12 oz. each) white baking chips
- 3 Tbsp. shortening
  Toppings: Grated coconut, grated chocolate and assorted sprinkles

DIRECTIONS

1. Line the bottom of a 9-in. springform pan with parchment; coat paper and sides of pan with cooking spray.
2. In a large bowl, beat cream cheese and sugar until smooth. Beat in sour cream and vanilla until blended. Add eggs; beat on low speed just until combined. Pour into prepared pan.
3. Place pan on a baking sheet. Bake at 350° for 45-50 minutes or until center is almost set. Cool on a wire rack for 10 minutes. Carefully run a knife around edge of pan to loosen; cool 1 hour longer. Cover and freeze overnight.
4. Remove from freezer and let stand for 30 minutes. Place cracker crumbs in a shallow bowl. Working quickly, scoop out 1-in. balls of cheesecake; roll each in cracker crumbs and insert a lollipop stick. Place on waxed paper-lined baking sheets. Freeze for 1 hour or until firm.
5. In a microwave, melt white chips and shortening at 70% power; stir until smooth. Place toppings in shallow bowls. Dip cheesecake pops in white chip mixture; allow excess to drip off. Roll in toppings. Place on waxed paper. Store in refrigerator.

1 CAKE POP 203 cal., 14g fat (8g sat. fat), 37mg chol., 80mg sod., 18g carb. (16g sugars, 0 fiber), 3g pro.

Orange Buttermilk Cupcakes

Simple and delicious, this is our all-time favorite dessert. You'll be surprised how the citrus flavor comes through in every bite.

—*Kim Chester, Cartersville, GA*

Prep **20 min.** ◆ Bake **20 min. + cooling** ◆ Makes **9 servings**

WHAT YOU'LL NEED

- **3** Tbsp. butter, softened
- ⅓ cup packed brown sugar
- ¼ cup sugar blend
- **1** tsp. grated orange zest
- **1** large egg,
  room temperature
- **1** large egg white,
  room temperature
- **2** Tbsp. plus 2½ tsp.
  orange juice, divided
- 1¼ cups cake flour
- ¾ tsp. baking powder
- ¼ tsp. baking soda
- ¼ tsp. salt
- ¼ tsp. ground ginger
- ½ cup buttermilk
- ½ cup confectioners' sugar

DIRECTIONS

1. In a large bowl, beat the butter, brown sugar, sugar blend and orange zest. Beat in the egg, egg white and 2 Tbsp. orange juice. Combine the flour, baking powder, baking soda, salt and ginger; gradually add to butter mixture alternately with buttermilk, beating well after each addition.

2. Coat 9 muffin cups with cooking spray or use paper liners; fill three-fourths full with batter. Bake at 350° for 18-20 minutes or until a toothpick inserted in the center comes out clean. Cool for 5 minutes before removing from pan to a wire rack to cool completely.

3. In a small bowl, combine confectioners' sugar and remaining orange juice. Frost cupcakes.

1 CUPCAKE 201 cal., 5g fat (3g sat. fat), 35mg chol., 208mg sod., 37g carb. (21g sugars, 0 fiber), 3g pro.

Confetti Cake with Brown Sugar Buttercream

This simple, festive cake is pure party fun.

—*Karen Berner, New Canaan, CT*

Prep **40 min.** ◆ Bake **20 min.** + cooling ◆ Makes **16 servings**

WHAT YOU'LL NEED

2¼ cups cake flour

1½ cups sugar

3½ tsp. baking powder

½ tsp. salt

½ cup unsalted butter, softened

4 large egg whites, room temperature

¾ cup 2% milk

1 tsp. clear vanilla extract

½ tsp. almond extract

⅓ cup rainbow jimmies

BUTTERCREAM

4 large egg whites

1 cup packed light brown sugar

¼ tsp. salt

1½ cups unsalted butter, softened

1½ tsp. clear vanilla extract

½ to ¾ tsp. yellow food coloring

Confetti sprinkles

DIRECTIONS

1. Preheat oven to 350°. Line bottoms of 2 greased 9-in. round baking pans with parchment; grease the parchment.

2. In a large bowl, whisk flour, sugar, baking powder and salt. Beat in butter. Add egg whites, 1 at a time, beating well after each addition. Gradually beat in milk and extracts. Gently fold in jimmies.

3. Transfer cake batter to prepared pans. Bake 20-25 minutes or until a toothpick inserted in center comes out clean. Cool in pans 10 minutes before removing to wire racks; remove paper. Cool completely.

4. For buttercream, in a heatproof bowl of a stand mixer, whisk egg whites, brown sugar and salt until blended. Place over simmering water in a large saucepan over medium heat. Whisking constantly, heat mixture until a thermometer reads 160°, 2-3 minutes.

5. Remove from heat. With whisk attachment of stand mixer, beat on high speed until stiff glossy peaks form, about 7 minutes.

6. Beat in butter, a few tablespoons at a time, on medium speed until smooth. Beat in vanilla and enough food coloring to achieve desired color.
7. Immediately spread frosting between layers and over top and sides of cake. Decorate with sprinkles. Store in refrigerator.

1 PIECE 436 cal., 24g fat (15g sat. fat), 62mg chol., 239mg sod., 51g carb. (36g sugars, 0 fiber), 4g pro.

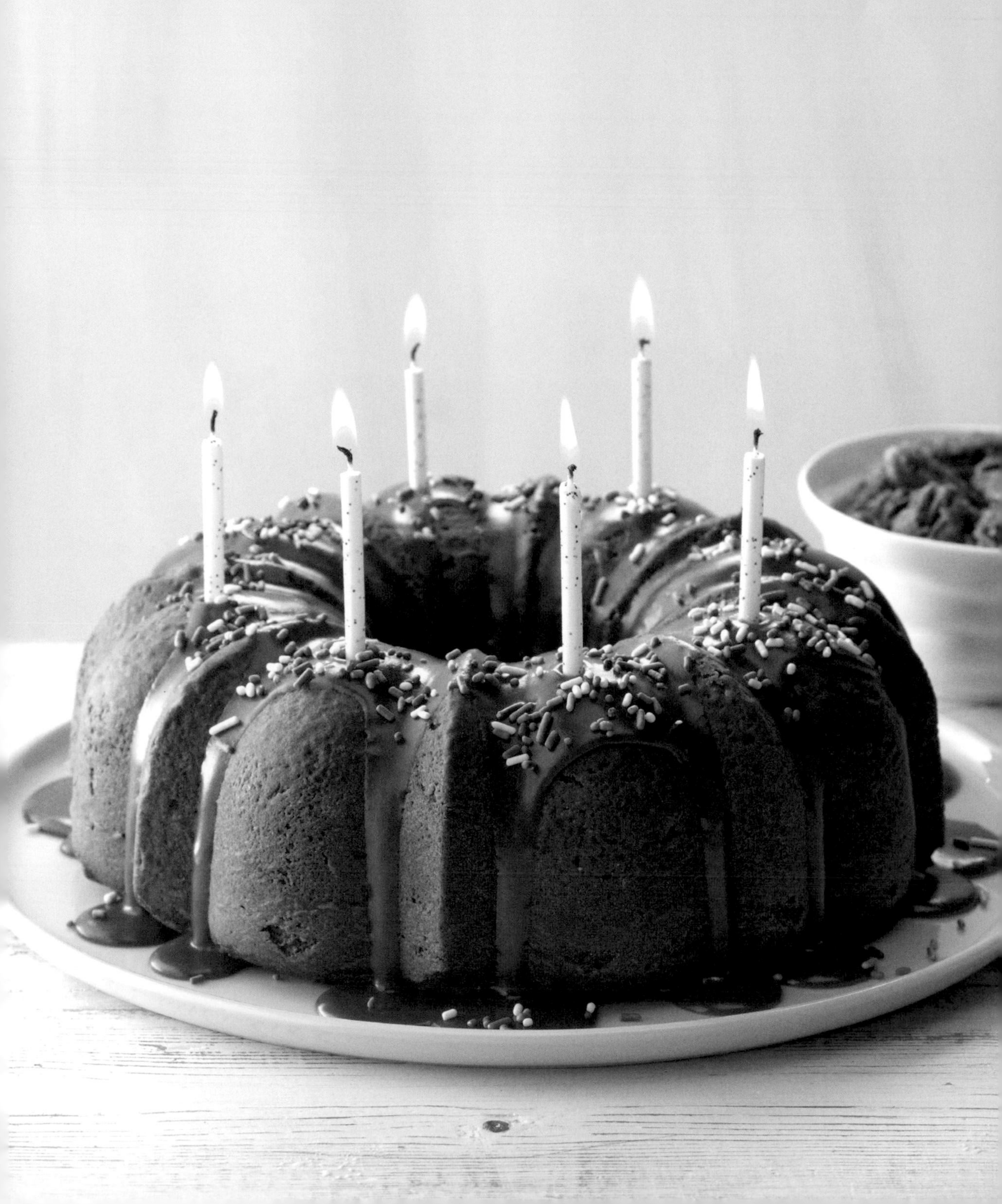

Heavenly Praline Cake

Filled with fabulous caramel, this cake also has a lovely icing.

—Jennifer Rodriguez, Midland, TX

Prep **40 min.** ◆ Bake **1 hour + cooling** ◆ Makes **16 servings (5 cups candied pecans)**

WHAT YOU'LL NEED

CANDIED PECANS

- 1 large egg white
- 4 cups pecan halves
- ⅓ cup sugar
- ⅓ cup packed dark brown sugar

CAKE

- 1 cup butter, softened
- 1 pkg. (8 oz.) cream cheese, softened
- 2 cups packed dark brown sugar
- 4 large eggs, room temperature
- 2 tsp. vanilla extract
- 2½ cups all-purpose flour
- 1 tsp. baking powder
- ½ tsp. baking soda
- ¼ tsp. salt
- 1 cup sour cream
- 1 cup chopped pecans, toasted

ICING

- 1 cup packed dark brown sugar
- ½ cup butter, cubed
- ¼ cup 2% milk
- 1 cup confectioners' sugar
- 1 tsp. vanilla extract

DIRECTIONS

1. Preheat oven to 325°. In a large bowl, beat egg white until foamy. Add pecan halves; stir gently to coat. Combine sugar and brown sugar; add to pecan mixture and stir gently to coat.

2. Spread into 2 greased 15x10x1-in. baking pans. Bake 18-22 minutes, stirring once. Cool. Store in an airtight container.

3. Meanwhile, in a large bowl, cream butter, cream cheese and brown sugar until light and fluffy. Add eggs, 1 at a time, beating well after each addition. Beat in vanilla. Combine flour, baking powder, baking soda and salt; add to the creamed mixture alternately with sour cream, beating well after each addition. Stir in chopped pecans.

4. Transfer to a greased and floured 10-in. fluted tube pan. Bake at 325° for 60-70 minutes or until a toothpick inserted in the center comes out clean. Cool 10 minutes before removing from pan to a wire rack to cool completely.

5. In a small saucepan, combine brown sugar, butter and milk. Bring to a boil; cook and stir 1 minute longer. Remove from heat; stir in confectioners' sugar and vanilla until smooth. Drizzle over cake. Serve with candied pecans.

1 PIECE 559 cal., 31g fat (17g sat. fat), 124mg chol., 305mg sod., 65g carb. (48g sugars, 1g fiber), 6g pro.

Poutine, You Say?

A celebratory birthday treat made to look like
a Canadian snack really takes the cake.

BY DONNA ZACHARIAS

When my daughters were young, I made them elaborate and creative birthday cakes. For my daughter Rhiannon's fourth birthday, I made a castle cake to go with her princess-themed party. It sounded better in theory than it ended up looking, but it gave me motivation to keep trying and to expand my ideas.

Eventually I had other successes. I did a three-tiered heart-shaped princess cake. There was a purse cake, complete with little accessories, and a couple of cakes with a beachy vibe. I also tried my hand at making flower marshmallow cupcakes—for which I used scissors to cut miniature marshmallows into "petals"—just like my mom used to make for special occasions. They required a lot of work but looked really beautiful.

As my daughters got older, life got busier and it seemed easier to purchase store-bought cakes for their birthdays. But recently, something inspired me to give cake-making another try.

A few days before Rhiannon's 19th birthday, we were sitting at the kitchen table discussing her past year away at a Bible college and all the exciting new experiences in her life. At one point she

started talking about how her favorite food, poutine, seemed to be present in so many fun events in her life, dates with her boyfriend and other outings.

She had been unable to come home for her 18th birthday, so we couldn't celebrate it with her. In a flash, I decided to design a cake for her 19th that looked like poutine!

Poutine, which originated in the Canadian province of Quebec, consists of french fries and cheese curds topped with brown gravy.

Far left: Rhiannon poses with her mom's special poutine cake on her 19th birthday. Top right: Donna made her daughters' birthdays memorable, such as when she made a purse cake and princess cake.

But when I went to Pinterest for some ideas, I realized I might be in over my head. I phoned a few local cake-makers to see if they could make the cake instead, but all were too busy. Eventually I found a bakery willing to make the "french fries" out of cookie dough, while I made my mom's go-to cake recipe for the base.

In the end, the cake actually came together surprisingly easily—and on the first try. The sugar cookie strips really did look like french fries; melted white chocolate doubled as cheese curds. For the finishing touch, Rhiannon drizzled "brown gravy," which was really butterscotch ice cream topping, over her "poutine."

Rhiannon was thrilled with the result, and I loved being able to create such a special, fun memory for her. ♦

Poutine Cake

My daughter was beyond thrilled with this cake!

—Donna Zacharias, Carrot River, SK

Prep **1 hour** ◆ Bake **30 min. + cooling** ◆ Makes **16 servings**

WHAT YOU'LL NEED

- 3 cups all-purpose flour
- 2 cups sugar
- ⅔ cup baking cocoa
- 2 tsp. baking soda
- 2 tsp. baking powder
- 1 tsp. salt
- 2 large eggs, room temperature
- ⅔ cup canola oil
- 2 tsp. vanilla extract
- 2 cups boiling water

BUTTERCREAM

- 1 cup unsalted butter, softened
- 1 tsp. 2% milk
- 1 tsp. vanilla extract
- ⅛ tsp. salt
- 3½ cups confectioners' sugar

ASSEMBLY

- 12 crisp ladyfinger cookies
- 8 oz. white candy coating, melted
- 2 cups butterscotch caramel ice cream topping

DIRECTIONS

1. Preheat oven to 350°. Line bottoms of 2 greased 8-in. round baking pans with parchment; grease the parchment.

2. In a large bowl, whisk flour, sugar, baking cocoa, baking soda, baking powder and salt. In another bowl, whisk eggs, oil and vanilla; stir into flour mixture. Stir in boiling water; batter will be thin.

3. Transfer to prepared pans. Bake until a toothpick inserted in center comes out clean, 30-35 minutes. Cool in pans 10 minutes before removing to wire racks; remove paper. Cool completely.

4. For frosting, in a large bowl, beat butter until creamy. Beat in milk, vanilla and salt. Gradually beat in confectioners' sugar until smooth. Spread frosting between cake layers, and over top and sides of cake. Using cookies, decorate cake as desired to look like french fries. Drop candy coating by tablespoonfuls to resemble cheese curds. Drizzle with ice cream topping to resemble gravy.

1 PIECE 719 cal., 28g fat (13g sat. fat), 65mg chol., 475mg sod., 114g carb. (81g sugars, 1g fiber), 6g pro.

My Amazing Ninth Birthday Party

Thanks to her talented mother,
one girl's birthday becomes a grand occasion.

BY ANEETA BROWN

If Martha Stewart had lived in my neighborhood in Kearney, Nebraska, as a little girl, she would have learned a thing or two simply by being a guest at my ninth birthday party in 1956. For this particular birthday, I was feted with a valentine theme.

My mother never met a paper plate or plastic cup that she liked. Ice cream was served in crystal dishes set on pottery plates, and even my 2-year-old sister (bottom right) drank her chocolate milk out of a glass. Candles, pipe cleaner dolls (made by Mother), and valentine cutouts decorated the tables. Foil party hats decorated the guests. Hidden among the crowd is my sister Marsha, age 10.

It was unthinkable that my mother would ever consider purchasing a bakery cake. She made an angel food cake, frosted with a confection that required sugar, egg whites, corn syrup, heat, a candy thermometer and an electric mixer. In the mid-1950s, children dressed in formal clothes for parties. My friend Linda Keiss (bottom left) wore a starched red dress with black velvet bows, and my brother Mark, age 6, looked comfortable in a necktie. My dress of polished cotton was made by my mother and featured covered buttons, embroidered yellow roses, scallops and piping around the collar.

My parents spent, without complaint, 3 cents postage for each invitation that was mailed. Georgia Spelt's daughter learned early in life that the most genuine form of invitation travels through the post office.

My mother's lasting gift to me was that, in addition to hosting my party (wearing high heels and a fashionable dress herself), she photographed the event with incomparable Kodachrome slide film. After almost 60 years, the colors are so rich that I can almost taste the strawberry ice cream. ♦

"My mother knew how to make every guest feel like royalty," says Aneeta Brown.

Craft Templates

Page 4
Spring: *Knotted Hanging Vase—A Lanyard Knot*

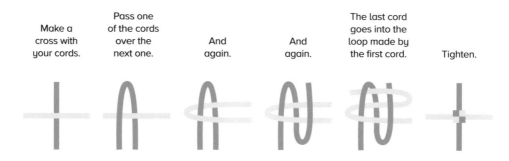

Make a cross with your cords.

Pass one of the cords over the next one.

And again.

And again.

The last cord goes into the loop made by the first cord.

Tighten.

Page 72
Mother's Day: *Seed Packet Wreath (scale 200%)*

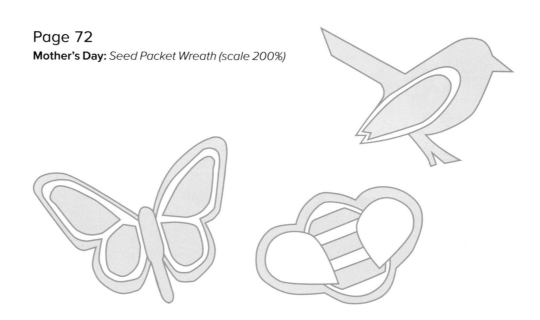

Page 194
Birthdays: *Gift-Wrap Organizer*

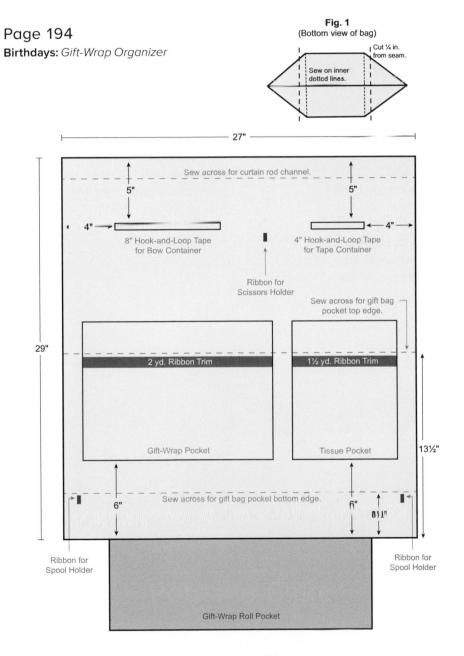

Fig. 1
(Bottom view of bag)

Cut ¼ in. from seam.

Sew on inner dotted lines.

27"

Sew across for curtain rod channel.

5"

5"

4"

4"

8" Hook-and-Loop Tape
for Bow Container

4" Hook-and-Loop Tape
for Tape Container

Ribbon for
Scissors Holder

Sew across for gift bag
pocket top edge.

29"

2 yd. Ribbon Trim

1½ yd. Ribbon Trim

Gift-Wrap Pocket

Tissue Pocket

13½"

Sew across for gift bag pocket bottom edge.

6"

6"

⅓11"

Ribbon for
Spool Holder

Ribbon for
Spool Holder

Gift-Wrap Roll Pocket

Craft Index

Recipe Index

Final Thought

A little country ingenuity can make even the plainest packages
feel special. When Andrew Ricchiuti's son celebrated his
first Easter, Andrew's mother, Catherine, got creative and
started a beloved family tradition that continues to
this day (featured on page 64).